Rekha

Rekha

The Untold Story

Yasser Usman

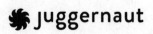

JUGGERNAUT BOOKS
KS House, 118 Shahpur Jat, New Delhi 110049, India

First published by Juggernaut Books 2016

ISBN 9788193284186

Typeset in Adobe Caslon Pro by R. Ajith Kumar, New Delhi

Printed at Manipal Technologies Ltd

For
Nazia, Myra
and
Rekha

Contents

Author's Note   ix

1. 'Basera'   1
2. Divorce   10
3. Witch Hunt   21
4. The Beginning   27
5. Bhanurekha   31
6. Bollywood Debut   40
7. The Kiss of 'Life'   48
8. 'Madrasan'   55
9. Vin Vin and Kin Kin   64
10. Didibhai   78
11. Makeover   88
12. Ghar   97
13. Zohrabai   102
14. The Other Woman   109
15. Queen   117
16. 'Silsila'   122

Contents

17. Love Triangle   131
18. Accident   138
19. Umrao   146
20. Arthouse   154
21. 'Lady Amitabh'   164
22. Suicide   169
23. Orphaned   177
24. Afterlife   183
25. Rajya Sabha   191
26. Farzana   196

Epilogue   204
Notes   206
Acknowledgements   218
Index   221
A Note on the Author   231

Author's Note

After my book on Rajesh Khanna was published in 2014, I kept getting handwritten letters and emails from die-hard fans of his. Some still find their way into my inbox. There was a common thread in all those letters: his fans were distressed, and surprised, to learn about Rajesh Khanna's loneliness, little known about before. Not only was he a regular at Bollywood mehfils but his colourful and energetic on-screen persona was difficult to reconcile with his loneliness. This made me want to take a closer look at the lives of popular film stars and what seems to be a common thread in them: a feeling of loneliness. That was why I wrote Rajesh Khanna's story. This is why I am writing this story.

I asked the film-maker Muzaffar Ali why he cast Rekha in *Umrao Jaan*, when there were arguably better actresses like Smita Patil around. Pat came the reply, 'Her eyes conveyed the experience of having been broken and then having pulled herself together. She has that strength, that striking feature which draws from her past.' Rekha's past is, indeed, shot through with sadness and stories of overcoming adversity.

From a troubled childhood during which she was unloved and unaccepted by her father to being pushed into the film industry that was not an easy place, to put it mildly, for a young girl; from the disturbing controversy about her being coerced into a kissing scene at age fourteen to her multiple failed relationships: there was no dearth of drama for Rekha as a child and young woman. These early experiences, perhaps, never left her. The film-maker Shyam Benegal told me, 'She was thirteen or fourteen when I did some ad films with her. She didn't know Hindi and yet she was in the Hindi film industry for some reason. But I can never forget that spark in her eyes and the confidence she had in front of the camera. That was something.' Despite the odds, Rekha clawed her way up in the cut-throat film industry.

When I was researching for this book, I interviewed people who had worked with Rekha or were close to her, personally and professionally. I was surprised that many of them reacted to this project with 'Why Rekha?' Several spoke about her in the most sexist of ways, called her unprintable names and ridiculed her relationships and affairs – always off the record, of course, when my dictaphone was switched off. Once the interview went on record, they made generic, platitudinous statements like 'It was great working with her', 'She is a fabulous actress', and dropped subtle, or not, hints about how she underwent a considerable transformation after she met 'him', referring to Amitabh Bachchan. Most were long interviews without anything substantial in them. In contrast, when I had interviewed the same people for my previous book, they shared numerous stories about Rajesh Khanna. In Rekha's case, there was an odd reluctance. Perhaps people were overwhelmed by the dominant love angle of her story, or maybe it was the habitual bias against women achievers at play. Of course, there were also those who let their guard down, like Gulzar, Shyam Benegal, Muzaffar Ali and several journalists who had been close to Rekha at some point or the other.

As a TV producer and journalist, I have seen numerous features on Rekha's alleged involvement with 'The Superstar'. Every year at the major film award functions, the cameras cut to Rekha when Amitabh Bachchan is on stage, and vice versa. Their supposed relationship is always at the centre of a discussion on Rekha. The fact that she is an award-winning actress in her own right and has worked in more than 150 films, a staggering number by any reckoning, takes a back seat. In an industry where heroines have a short shelf life, Rekha continued to play the lead for two decades. But the national interest in her love life that has sustained for more than forty years has always trumped and overshadowed interest in her career.

She is, of course, partly responsible for this – for instance, Rekha herself publicly credits even her miraculous makeover in the 1970s to Amitabh Bachchan.

I have to admit that I am not a huge fan of Rekha's. I grew up in the 1980s when her career was on the downslide. But I certainly love some of her performances from that decade and have always especially enjoyed her interviews. Her current carefully cultivated reclusive and withdrawn public persona, though, is in sharp contrast to her old uninhibited interviews which have been painstakingly recollected throughout this book.

When I started writing this book, I naturally tried to reach out to Rekha for a meeting and an interview. Several calls were made to her official landline number. Gulzar even tried to help me by putting in a good word. Then, one morning, I got a phone call from her secretary, Farzana. She politely asked me what I was writing about. I explained my vision for the project: to present Rekha's *true* story and requested an appointment with her. Farzana graciously heard me out, we had a nice chat and she told me that she'd get back to me. That call never came. I tried phoning multiple times, only to be greeted by a message on an answering machine – yes, she still uses one. I gave up.

Would this book have had another dimension had Rekha agreed to speak with me? Perhaps, but I doubt it. After the 1990 suicide of her husband, Mukesh Agarwal, the tone of Rekha's interviews changed considerably.

Unlike her previous blithe and straightforward answers, she became reserved. I can't imagine she would have said anything substantially different from what she's already said in her more recent measured and guarded manner.

Rekha seems to have consciously decided to cultivate an image of a reclusive 'diva'. Her interviews have become philosophical and abstract. Millennials think of her as retiring and distant. But how did she get there? Who is the real Rekha? Is she the mysterious and elusive woman of the years after her doomed marriage? Or the carefree and loudmouthed teenager who never shied away from speaking her mind? Is she the product of her association with Amitabh Bachchan? Is there more to the story of Bollywood's 'eternal other woman'?

To find answers to these questions we have to go back into her past, into her childhood and early setback-filled years in Bollywood before she became the recluse we know today. That is where her story is hidden.

1

'Basera'

'How will I spot the right man? By looking into his eyes. I am a good face reader. My intuition seldom goes wrong. The moment I see the right guy I'll know.' – Rekha[1]

Metamorphosis is a rite of time. The caterpillar transforms into a butterfly; Madras becomes the cosmopolitan Chennai; Bombay becomes Mumbai; Bhanurekha Ganesan becomes the glamorous Rekha. Each is far removed from its origins. Yet essentially, at core, unaltered. We will be visiting each of these cities, for they resonate with stories from the past. Stories of the woman whose love and life have captivated national interest for more than four decades. But first we go to Delhi, for that is where the phoenix rose from the ashes.

Here is her story.

Even before liberalization, the rich and elite of Delhi

1

had started to spill further south into Chhatarpur, famous for a temple by the same name. In the late 1980s, if you drove past the Qutub Minar and turned into Gadaipur district, a dirt road would have led you through rows of farms until you reached a simple sign that said 'Basera' (abode).

As the gates opened, you were transported into a private little dreamworld, a sanctuary, where you were confronted by a split-level home of stone and glass built on a hill, surrounded by greenery. This was the residence of Mukesh Agarwal.

Born into a middle-class Bania family, Mukesh had abandoned studying at the age of thirteen. For many years he did odd jobs. Then, in the late 1970s, at the age of twenty-four, he started a company of his own that manufactured kitchenware under the brand name Hotline.

Sifting through the pages of Mukesh's past, I came upon Neeraj Kumar, Mukesh's one-time friend. A retired Indian Police Service officer, Neeraj Kumar had served as Delhi's commissioner of police. Mukesh's and Neeraj Kumar's paths had crossed at the time that Hotline made ripples in Delhi due to its success. According to Neeraj Kumar, 'Mukesh Agarwal belonged to that breed of entrepreneurs who made it big at a time when others had not emerged. All these start-up scenarios had not happened.'

From an ordinary background, Mukesh had always wanted to break into the circles of Delhi's elite. Craving for social prominence, he threw lavish parties for Delhi's socialites. He made it a point to invite every film celebrity who happened to be in town. Neeraj Kumar remembers Mukesh as a 'very nice guy, very kind, but he had a complex. The complex was that he wanted to show that he has arrived. He did not believe in keeping a low profile.' Mukesh was known for his eccentricities; he'd do practically anything to catch a celebrity's eye. Neeraj Kumar said, 'He bought a horse and he had a farmhouse in Mehrauli. When he was expecting a guest, he would mount the horse and sit there waiting!' This was no ordinary horse; it was, in fact, an enormous stallion. Perhaps his gimmicks worked because, in Neeraj Kumar's words, 'He had befriended a whole lot of Bollywood actors and actresses. He knew Feroz Khan, Sanjay Khan. Perhaps this thing about the horse was taken from Feroz Khan.'[2]

It was Mukesh's long-standing desire to hobnob with celebrities and somehow become part of the film industry.

~

There was a time in Delhi when the glamorous Rekha and the famous fashion designer and socialite Bina Ramani would catch up with each other often. Over one such meeting,[3] Rekha expressed a desire to get married and to settle down. All she sought then was a man who could be her partner for life.

It was early 1990. One evening, Rekha's phone rang.

It was Bina Ramani from Delhi. She wanted Rekha to talk to her 'crazy fan'. Bina told Rekha that this crazy fan of hers was a well-known businessman from Delhi, and also a very good human being. 'His name is Mukesh Agarwal. Shall I give him your number?' Rekha told her not to. Instead, she took his number.

She probably wouldn't have guessed it then but this one phone call was going to change her life forever.

The story of Mukesh Agarwal's life was filmi, much like Rekha's. And, like her, he too had failed to find a lasting companion in life. Perhaps their paths were destined to cross.

~

Rekha recollected later that 'Bina Ramani had introduced him to me. At first, I was totally disinterested in him. When Bina goaded me on, I phoned him.'[4]

The first conversation between them was formal but it is said that Mukesh was completely enamoured by Rekha's husky voice. He was also over the moon that a woman worshipped by millions in India had rung him up. Rekha had taken the first step.

A series of phone calls between the two then followed. Rekha's Delhi-based friend Surinder Kaur was witness to this relationship since its beginning. Surinder was an air hostess and was very close to Rekha at that time. She wanted to see Rekha settled down. Bina and Surinder repeatedly coaxed Rekha: 'He is a great guy...don't let this chance go by.'

Rekha and Mukesh met for the first time in Bombay within a month of their first phone call. For Rekha, tired of the pretences and demands of showbiz, Mukesh was a pleasant change. His simple and honest demeanour signalled a rare genuineness to her. Clearly star-struck, Mukesh paid her dazzling compliments, something that Rekha had always loved. He left no stone unturned in wooing her, and lavished her with affection. As with everything else in his life, Mukesh went overboard.

He persuaded Rekha to visit Delhi, and she did. Soon, she stood at the centre of attention in his sprawling farmhouse in Chhatarpur, Basera. This was a welcome change from the glitz of Bombay. One could easily get used to the fawning respect, adulation and attention she got. A bond grew between the two of them: he loved her queen-diva image and she loved his till-death-do-us-part devotion.

Bina Ramani said in an interview that Rekha and Mukesh met a few times though Rekha herself recalled: 'I had met him just once before marriage, then met him once at Bina's. That's about it. It was Surinder who persuaded me to meet him again. I met the family in Delhi. I liked the people. They looked very simple. Mitho Bhabhiji [Mukesh's elder brother Anil Gupta's wife] totally won me over.'[5] Mukesh's sister-in-law once told him, *Hamare ghar hoor aayi hai.* (An angel has visited our home.) You must be proud of her.'[6] This was the acceptance that Rekha was looking for.

Mukesh had a close friend in Bombay, the actress Deepti Naval. Ever since their meeting at a common friend's house in Delhi in 1981, they had been good friends. Deepti recalled, 'After he spoke to Rekha on the phone and the two met in Bombay and again in Delhi, Mukesh couldn't stop talking about her. He used to gush about her... I thought he was totally bonkers over her.'

Rekha and Mukesh didn't ponder over each other's past. They didn't think too much about the future. Nothing mattered but that present, pressing feeling of love.

~

Sunday, 4 March 1990. It had been just over a month since Rekha and Mukesh had first met. He was restless. Noon found him sitting in Rekha's house along with Surinder Kaur. Without preamble, he proposed marriage.

'Surinder goaded me into saying yes to Mukesh when he came over to Bombay again,' Rekha said recalling that day.[7] Mukesh couldn't control his excitement. Jumping up with joy he said, 'Let's get married right away!' Neither of their families were in Bombay; still, they decided that the wedding had to take place that very day.

It was as if they were scared that if not then, it might not happen at all.

Rekha was finally getting married. When evening fell,

she wore her favourite red-and-gold Kanjeevaram sari with exquisite jewellery. Along with Surinder, they set out in search of a temple in Juhu. They found a temple but there was no priest inside. Some distance ahead was the Iskon temple, but it was incredibly crowded. In front of it, however, was another temple: Mukteshwar Devalaya. The junior temple priest, Sanjay Bodas, had already gone to sleep in his little room behind the temple. Mukesh woke him up and told him that he had to get married immediately. The confused priest looked at Rekha and was stunned. It's not every day that such a well-known face appeared at his temple. And that too to get married urgently, without the customary entourage. He was dazed and, perhaps, the wedding party was too. Though the temple was not allowed to be opened after the evening aarti, and the priest was not supposed to solemnize the wedding, the rules were broken that night. (The priest was later barred from the temple.)

At about 10.30 at night, the wedding mantras were chanted, and Rekha and Mukesh exchanged the ritual garlands. Thirty-seven-year-old Mukesh and thirty-five-year-old Rekha were now man and wife.

The world suddenly felt more accommodating to Rekha Agarwal.

After a lifetime of seeking, Rekha, born out of wedlock, had finally got what she most desired: a legitimate surname.

~

7

After the ceremony, the glamour-obsessed Mukesh suggested that they visit a few of his film-star friends. But Rekha turned down his idea to visit Akbar and Sanjay Khan. 'Let's visit Hemaji,' she is said to have suggested. Rekha and Hema Malini's friendship went back a decade. The newly-weds, with Surinder in tow, dropped in at Hema Malini's house. Dharmendra was there too. 'Don't tell me you married this guy!' Hema Malini remarked softly in Tamil. 'Yes, of course,' replied Rekha. 'Is he very rich?' was the next question. Rekha did not answer that time.[8]

The next morning, Deepti Naval got a phone call from Rekha. 'Guess what? I have become your bhabhi!' Rekha exclaimed. Deepti was confused. Rekha continued excitedly, 'I am Rekha Agarwal now. I've married Mukesh. Isn't he like a brother to you?' 'I couldn't believe it for a while,' Deepti recalled.[9] Twenty-four hours later they were in London for their honeymoon.

The initial days in London were beautiful. That was the first time that Rekha and Mukesh had spent so much time together. But it took only a week for Rekha to realize that they were very different people. She was also shocked to see Mukesh taking several pills a day. Still, she thought, now that they had to spend the rest of their lives together, such matters would have to be overlooked. 'I've to make [a] success of it,' she told herself. 'Can Rekha fail in anything she attempts?'[10]

They had been in London for more than a week. Rekha could see that something was troubling Mukesh. And then, one day, a gloomy Mukesh looked deep into her eyes and said, 'There's an AB in my life too.'

2

Divorce

'I'll quit only when I'm pregnant.' – Rekha

While everybody knew who Rekha's AB was, the AB in Mukesh Agarwal's life was Akash Bajaj. She was his psychotherapist and had been treating him for the last ten years. She had also been involved with him personally. Neeraj Kumar remembered, 'Mukesh was a chronic patient of depression and, if I'm not wrong, it ran in his family.' Mukesh's sister and a few other members of his family had suffered from depression, making him genetically predisposed to the condition. His was a severe case, and it was Akash who was responsible for him getting better. Neeraj Kumar remarked, 'She had kind of nursed him back from [the] absolute brink of despair.'[1]

The despair that Neeraj Kumar alluded to was caused by a previous failed relationship. During the early 1980s, Mukesh was seriously involved with a wannabe starlet,

Kitty Malkan. They were about to get married when Kitty abruptly decided to leave him and follow her dreams in the film industry.

The humiliation was unbearable for Mukesh and he attempted to kill himself. During this dark phase, he met Akash Bajaj, a divorcee. Remembering their first meeting, Akash said, 'I had met him when I was doing my internship at Kothari nursing home. Mukesh was a very depressed man in those days as he had just broken up with Kitty, with whom he had a long-standing relationship. Slowly we became great friends. He used to come over to my place often and would play badminton with my daughters.'[2]

They soon became lovers and theirs turned into a very emotional relationship. 'They used to virtually live together and they were a pair. It was also believed that he was supporting her financially to a large extent. It was an open secret,' according to Neeraj Kumar. Mukesh had become an important part of the lives of Akash and her teenaged daughters, Monisha and Anjali. They used to go on holidays together like any happy family.

But despite the intensity of their relationship, and the fact that they had been together for nine years, Mukesh had no qualms about rushing off to marry Rekha without saying a word to Akash. He didn't think twice before proposing to Rekha. News of this came as a shock to Akash: 'Mukesh had offered marriage to me but I had put it off saying that I didn't want to burden him with a readymade family. In fact, I told him to get married and have a family of his own but his marriage to Rekha came as a surprise to me and all his other friends. I was not just shocked but extremely concerned for him.'[3]

~

Back in Bombay, Rekha and Mukesh threw a small party for close friends to celebrate their wedding. Mukesh was then going through a phase of depression. According to Neeraj Kumar, 'I clearly remember it was Santa Cruz Centaur Hotel. Mukesh was on [the] phone line with me, saying that "Neeraj, I'm going to jump off!"' Mukesh's depression had been manifesting in strong suicidal tendencies. Neeraj Kumar tried to talk him out of it, and reminded him of his recent wedding. 'He felt there was no meaning to his life and he wanted to end it. This had been a regular occurrence with Mukesh and was getting tiresome for people close to him,'[4] remembered Neeraj Kumar.

Meanwhile, Rekha had been giving interviews in which she proclaimed Mukesh as the love of her life. 'My first reaction to his name – "Mukesh Agarwal" – it didn't have that ring of romance to it. It was so far removed from what I had ever dreamt of. But today Mukesh Agarwal is the name for me,' Rekha said.[5] A film with Rekha in the lead was released around that time, *Azaad Desh Ke Gulam*, a rather misleading name for an action suspense thriller. Rekha was in the news again.

On 15 April 1990, Rekha and Mukesh had another wedding ceremony, replete with Vedic rites, at the famous Tirupati temple, in the presence of Rekha's mother, Pushpavalli. But more important for Rekha was the attendance of her father, Gemini Ganesan, who came with his film-maker friend Raghavendra Rao to bless his estranged daughter.

It seemed to be an auspicious new beginning.

~

Leaving her city and her friends behind, Rekha had started spending the weekends in Delhi. Though 'Mrs Agarwal' did not have a glamorous ring to it, her new name and identity were like balm on an old wound. Mukesh and Rekha were among the most talked about couples of that time. These were moments of bliss. Indeed, Rekha gave interviews saying her marriage had given a new dimension to her life. She loved the sense of togetherness: 'A silent glance…a touch…a casual compliment like "you're looking so fresh" or "you look so different today, so new"…adds so much to living.'[6] Even though *Azaad Desh Ke Gulam* tanked at the box office, Rekha's personal life gave her reason to smile.

Rekha started enjoying her new life at Basera. 'It's

been my dream to move away from the bustle of the city to a small world surrounded by greens...trees, flowers... I am arriving closer to that dream with him [Mukesh],' she had said.[7]

One evening, Rekha and Mukesh went over to Neeraj Kumar's place in Chanakyapuri. He remembers that Rekha was dressed like any girl next door, in a simple salwaar kameez. 'We had a small dance party, just four–five of us, and she danced with us. We have pictures from that lovely evening. She also came into the bedroom and sat on the bed as if, you know, she had known us for ages and we also felt that we had known her for ages.'[8]

The glow of the relationship held for a few more months, till the reality of life caught up with the couple. On her weekend visits to Delhi, Rekha would often find that Mukesh had plans to party. Though desperate to spend some alone time with her husband, she found herself mostly surrounded by loud crowds. These incidents made her feel like she was probably nothing more than a trophy wife for Mukesh, who constantly wanted to show her off to the world. The two, of course, were the talk of the town, and Mukesh left no opportunity to flaunt Rekha, have her by his side. 'They spent some happy times together in the beginning. But when the fights began, it was something more than what usually takes place between husband and wife,' Mukesh's brother Anil Gupta said later.

The year they got married, 1990, saw a worldwide

financial crisis and Mukesh too suffered setbacks in his business, though he kept Rekha in the dark about them. When she found out, disillusionment set in. Cracks were beginning to appear in their marriage. Mukesh was a man of extremes, and Rekha was only just beginning to realize this. A mere two months after their wedding, Rekha's visits to Delhi started becoming infrequent. Mukesh couldn't bear her long absences and even wanted her to stop working in films, a demand that was not just irrational but violated their agreement at the time of the wedding. 'I'll quit only when I'm pregnant,' Rekha had told Mukesh.[9]

∼

The Mukesh who had appeared mature and sincere at the beginning of their association now behaved like a teenaged fan. When Rekha cut down on her visits to Delhi, Mukesh began spending more time in Bombay. Rather than paying attention to his failing business, he idled away time on Rekha's shoots and at Bollywood parties. Acquaintances would often ask Rekha in disbelief: was this the guy she had married? Mukesh's behaviour was becoming a source of embarrassment for Rekha, but he didn't realize it. Obsessed with the glitz of Tinseltown, he just couldn't help himself.

Mukesh's almost neurotic eagerness to rub shoulders with the rich and famous would mortify Rekha. Once he insisted that she introduce him to Rajiv Gandhi when they were passing his farmhouse. 'Let's drop by to say hello to him. I need to cultivate important people,'[10] he said. 'I know him but he is not a friend,' replied Rekha, and firmly refused to indulge Mukesh. Later he wanted her to fly down with him to Gwalior for a cricket match that was being organized by Madhavrao Scindia. 'Let's meet Scindia, he can be very useful for my business,' said Mukesh, who was setting up a factory in Gwalior. 'Please don't involve me in your business deals,' Rekha protested. Mukesh was offended. 'Isn't my business your concern as well?' he asked. Their different points of view led to friction. There were ego clashes. Their incompatibility was becoming glaringly obvious.

~

Three months into the marriage, the magnitude of her folly dawned on Rekha. But she had gone to town boasting about her happily married status. She had painted Mukesh as an ideal life partner in many interviews. What was she going to tell everyone now?

Rekha had always been tempted by the idea of marriage but it hadn't lived up to her expectations. She had made the man of her dreams out to be larger than life and married life some kind of utopia. But the truth was starkly different. Her husband was fallible. He was taking heavy medication for acute depression, something that Rekha had been unaware of. Also, after the honeymoon period, the banality of marriage couldn't match up to the rush that stardom and the associated glitz brought to Rekha's life. The title of Mrs Agarwal was fast losing its sheen. Was this what she had yearned for all these years? All of a sudden, Rekha couldn't fathom why.

Her mind must have been churning with confusion. She took a step back from the all-consuming relationship, and bought some time to think things through. But when making sense of the situation proved to be too difficult, she started distancing herself from Mukesh and his family. She stopped taking his phone calls.

For a depressed Mukesh, this came as a huge blow. It may have even revived the pain of betrayal he had felt when Kitty abandoned him. With all means of communication to Rekha blocked, he started talking to the media. Reports of chinks in their relationship found their way into various publications, with headlines like 'Rekha Exposed' and 'The Shocking Past of Rekha's Husband'.[11] The impact of his actions, however, was the exact opposite of what he had hoped: Rekha receded into her shell and pushed him further away. Whatever trust and faith she had had in Mukesh was now completely shattered. She distanced herself totally and this made Mukesh even more anxious. He started pursuing her obsessively. He called her incessantly, and begged and cried to have her back.

In his desperation to see her, Mukesh flew down to Bombay. His sister-in-law, Anil Gupta's wife, went with him. They tried calling Rekha from their hotel but according to Mukesh's sister-in-law, she never came on the line. Finally, they decided to go to Rekha's house at Bandstand.

There they met Farzana, Rekha's ever-faithful secretary. In the film industry, it is common knowledge that Rekha doesn't do a thing without Farzana's consent and approval. Farzana manages Rekha's career, home and, according to some, her life. 'Why do you get humiliated like this?' Farzana is supposed to have asked Mukesh and his sister-in-law. 'She will not meet you and, anyway, she's not in.' Just then, a guard came in to inform Farzana that Rekha had come home. Mukesh rushed down, his sister-in-law behind him. As he reached the gate, Rekha saw him and immediately turned around, sat back in her car and drove off. Mukesh is said to have run after her, crying and sobbing, pleading with her to stop. 'It was raining that night,' Mukesh's sister-in-law reportedly told Deepti Naval. 'Mukesh was drenched and there were tears running down his cheeks. He screamed himself hoarse but the woman did not turn back to look even once.'[12]

For Rekha, this relationship had reached the point of no return. Divorce papers were being prepared in Bombay.

Rekha was trying to channel her thoughts and energies into her acting career. She was shooting for Sunil Dutt's social drama *Yeh Aag Kab Bujhegi* (1991) and *Sheshnaag* (1990), a film based on the then successful formula of shape-shifting snakes. Meanwhile, the oddly titled

Mera Pati Sirf Mera Hai (1990), directed by Manobala, had Rekha playing the role of the 'other woman'. The film, a remake of the Tamil *En Purushanthaan Enakku Mattumthaan* (1989), had Jeetendra and Radhika in the lead roles. When the title of a film translates to 'My husband is mine alone', you know you're in for some ridiculous melodrama, and that's exactly what audiences got. An average earner, the film got added to Rekha's long list of forgettable staple Bollywood fare.

In August 1990, it was reported that, in a state of depression, Mukesh had tried to commit suicide by overdosing on sleeping pills. The headline in *Stardust* magazine screamed 'How Rekha Drove Mukesh to Attempt Suicide'. Rekha is said to have called him after the incident and said, 'If a marriage doesn't work, you can do nothing about it. I am not the kind who'll stick on under false pretences. What's the point in prolonging a relationship which has no future?'[13]

It is not possible to fully know what goes on in the private life of a couple, but it's easy to take sides on the basis of half information, without knowing the actual play of emotions, words, actions and egos. Should Rekha have honoured her commitment at the cost of her peace of mind? Should she have continued living with Mukesh despite their obvious differences? Would this have ensured he wouldn't try to commit suicide again? Was Rekha shying away from her responsibility to her husband and her home?

Neeraj Kumar recalled, 'It was not as if the marriage to Rekha at any stage revived him or rejuvenated his mind. He never felt really happy I guess, because the disease was something, you know, an inner psychological condition.' He alleged that Mukesh had attempted suicide on several occasions, and failed. Once he tried to drown himself in his own swimming pool but his staff saw him and pulled him out. It was becoming difficult for Mukesh's friends and family to counsel him on a daily basis. 'Eventually, what happened was that I began to get irritated whenever I got news that Mukesh had attempted suicide because every second [or] third day either he used to call [to say] that he feels like dying or news of his suicide attempt would arrive.'

Mukesh was desperate, frustrated and chronically depressed. On 10 September 1990, when Mukesh called Rekha she took his call. They talked and agreed to get divorced by mutual consent, just six months into their marriage. On 26 September, Rekha left for America to be part of a stage show.

The dream had cracked and shattered. The companions, after walking together some distance, were ready to part ways. But the road that Mukesh chose to tread left a deep wound on everyone's hearts.

3

Witch Hunt

'She's become the national vamp.' – Anupam Kher

On 2 October 1990, nearly seven months after his marriage to Rekha, Mukesh seemed rather happy. 'He woke up early in the morning and came to lie down in my room. We had breakfast together. He even told my wife to prepare some lunch as he'd be coming home at about 1.30 p.m.,' Mukesh's brother Anil Gupta recalled.[1] He left home to meet his close friend Akash Bajaj. Then he went to his farmhouse, Basera. Smiling, he told his cook that he was famished and asked for his favourite dishes to be made. 'I am going to sleep in my room. Do not wake me up till the food is ready,' Mukesh reportedly said and retired to his room.

The room was alive with memories of Rekha. Mukesh may have been trying to hide the pain of these memories behind his cheerful demeanour. Maybe he was trying to conceal what he intended to do.

He picked up Rekha's dupatta and fashioned a noose out of it. Climbing on top of his bed, he tied one end of the dupatta to the ceiling fan, pulled the noose around his neck and hanged himself. It is said that Mukesh could have saved himself if he wanted. All he needed to do was put his feet back on the bed. But he curled his legs and choked the last breath out of his lungs, till his body became limp.

There was a determination and finality to this attempt, a resolve perhaps drawn from a series of failed suicide attempts, or maybe his failed relationships, we'll never know.

Neeraj Kumar was then deputy commissioner of police (south). He was home when news of Mukesh's death reached him. He also heard that Mukesh's body had been taken away by his family to his brother's bungalow at 3 Flagstaff Road, Civil Lines. 'Now, that worried me because the suicide had been committed in Mehrauli and the body had been taken to Civil Lines and apparently nobody in my district or in Mehrauli police station knew about the incident except me.' Being the DCP, this put him in an awkward situation. If Mukesh's body were cremated without a post-mortem, it would likely spark off a controversy. 'I reached Civil Lines, and took his brother Anil Gupta aside,' Neeraj shared. He told Anil that he had come to take the body away. Anil was shocked, and said that that would cause even more distress to the family. 'That's your problem, but I have to take the body away. This has to be subject to [a] post-mortem because it is an unnatural death. It's a suicide,' said Neeraj, adding that matters in this case were complicated because Mukesh was married to a famous actress.

Matters, indeed, came to a head, especially for that famous actress.

~

Earlier, in 1986, the fantasy film *Nagina*, where Sridevi played an *ichchhadhari nagin*, shape-shifting snake, proved to be a mammoth blockbuster, catapulting her to superstardom. *Nagina* was one of the first Bollywood films of this era to have a genuine sequel. On various occasions, Sridevi had appreciated the advice that Rekha had given her on diction, make-up, etc., which had greatly helped her when she was starting out in films.

With *Sheshnaag* (1990), Rekha also jumped on to the nagin bandwagon. Her song with Jeetendra, *'Humein Aasmaan Ne Bheja'*, had been received well, and there was hope that the film would also do well. *Sheshnaag* was a big-budget film, with Rishi Kapoor, Anupam Kher and Madhavi also playing important roles.

A little after its release, Mukesh's death made headlines. People started to blacken Rekha's face on *Sheshnaag* posters. At some places, they even threw dung at it.

And so started a national witch hunt.

~

'Rekha didn't come for the last rites or cremation. I think, by then, she had already kind of switched off,' said Neeraj Kumar. Rekha heard about Mukesh's death in New York, where she had gone for a stage show. She immediately made a phone call to Anil Gupta's wife, whom she called Mitho bhabhiji, who said, *'Tum apna dhyaan rakhna* [you take care of yourself], we are all with you.' But this wasn't to be so.

The press lapped up the sensational story of Mukesh's suicide and featured reports with outrageous headlines like 'The Black Widow' (*Showtime*, November 1990) and 'The Macabre Truth behind Mukesh's Suicide' (*Cine Blitz*, November 1990). Delhi high society and Bombay's film industry vociferously condemned Rekha for 'murdering' Mukesh Agarwal. His mother's wail made headlines when she cried, *'Woh daayan mere bete ko kha gayi. Bhagwan use kabhi maaf nahi karega.'*[2] (That witch devoured my son. God will never forgive her.)

An angry Anil Gupta said, 'My brother loved Rekha truly. For him love was a do or die attempt. He could not tolerate what Rekha was doing to him. Now what does she want, does she want our money?'[3]

Akash Bajaj, too, remarked, 'I am angry at his death and absolutely furious with the person who caused this to him. I want to lash out and ask why?'[4]

Deepti Naval pitched in, 'She does not even realise that in Mukesh she lost the only one person in the world who had accepted her for whatever her past and whatever she was. Who loved her like no one ever had.' Deepti broke down, 'I had seen him pleading over the phone with Farzana to call Rekha on the line. He was sobbing like a baby. "Please…please let me talk to her." And you know what Farzana had to say? "Sorry, her lawyers have instructed her not to talk to you." I am not saying that it was Rekha's fault only. I mean I don't know anything, [but] Rekha could have been a little more sensitive towards him.'[5]

The reaction of the film fraternity was vociferous: 'Rekha has put such a blot on the face of the film industry that it'll be difficult to wash it away easily. I think after this any respectable family will think twice before accepting any actress as their *bahoo*,' said Subhash Ghai.[6] 'It's going to be tough even professionally for her. No conscientious director will work with her ever again. How will the audience accept her as *Bharat ki nari* or *insaf ki devi*?' Subhash Ghai added.

'She's become the national vamp. Professionally and personally, I think it's curtains for her. I mean I don't know how will I react to her if I come face to face with her,' said Anupam Kher,[7] her co-star in several films of that time.

The national obsession with Rekha's love life had overnight morphed into a national hatred for her. She was branded a witch, a heartless man-eater who did not think twice before killing her husband. There was no future for her, it was deemed. She had no major films in hand, and the industry was unanimous that it didn't want her back. Her fans didn't seem to want her either and *Sheshnaag* was an enormous flop. Rekha was projected as a symbol of everything that was wrong and unacceptable in Indian society.

But like a phoenix she would rise again, for she had seen this before, been here before. She was an eternal survivor, an eternal fighter.

4

The Beginning

'Appa's *USP was that he had a way with women.*'
– Narayani Ganesh, Rekha's half-sister

While today's Chennai might take pride in the premium luxury hotel the Park, on the crossroads of Mount Road and Nungambakkam, people have not forgotten what used to stand there at that very spot: the famous Gemini Studios. One of the top movie studios in the country, its golden era spanned the 1940s and 1950s.

The magnificent double-door entrance to the Park is reminiscent of a theatre, and cinema is the underlying theme of its decor: vintage movie posters decorate the guest room walls and showcase Gemini Studios' hits. One of the hotel's restaurants is named 601, after the erstwhile studio's address. While walking the Park's corridors one can hear the echoes of many stories from the past. One

such story is that of Bhanurekha Ganesan. But in order
to tell it, we need to go back in time, to 1947.

~

Madras, 1947.

Tales of intimacy between the famous Gemini Studios
actress Pushpavalli and Gemini's owner, S.S. Vasan, were
reverberating in its hallways. A mother of two (a son,
Babuji, and daughter, Rama, from a previous relationship),
thirty-year-old Pushpavalli was an ambitious woman –
both in her career and in her love life. She was already the
star of Vasan's films but craved the status of his wife. Vasan,
who was already married, was happy to give Pushpavalli
anything she wanted, other than his name.

Around the same time, the heart and mind of a
dapper young chemistry lecturer at the famous Madras
Christian College had grown disinterested in formulae
and equations. He left his job to pursue a yearning for the
silver screen and joined Gemini Studios as a production
executive. As fate would have it, the young man got an
opportunity to do a small role in a Tamil film starring
Pushpavalli, *Miss Malini* (1947), an adaptation of a story
by the celebrated writer R.K. Narayan.

On the sets of the film, the lead actress and the former
chemistry lecturer started growing closer, right under the
nose of the producer, S.S. Vasan, or 'The Boss' as he was
commonly referred to. *Miss Malini* was a hit, and Vasan

decided to try to break into the Hindi film industry. With Pushpavalli as the heroine, he made the Hindi film *Sansar* in 1951, also a hit. The producer–actress duo started dreaming of making it big in Bombay. Vasan signed Dilip Kumar and Dev Anand for his dream project, a film called *Insaniyat*. It soon became the talk of the town.

Vasan wanted Pushpavalli to be cast as the heroine in this film. He knew that *Insaniyat* could prove to be a turning point for her and establish her as a big star in the Bombay film world. He had one condition, however: that Pushpavalli should pick between Vasan and the new lad.

She picked the new lad.

His name was Ramaswamy Ganesan.

~

Ramaswamy left Gemini Studios, but with a new identity. He adopted the name of the studio where he had begun his career. Ramaswamy Ganesan became Gemini Ganesan. In years to come, Gemini would become one of the biggest stars of Tamil cinema. He became popular as *kaadal mannan* or 'king of romance'. This sobriquet, however, applied more to Gemini's private life than to his professional life.

'We all had a great deal of respect for him and for each other. As an actor, *appa*'s USP was that he had a way with women; he oozed charm and with his candy-box good looks, wide-eyed innocence and gentle ways, he won over the hearts of more than a generation of fans. For them, he was the eternal romantic hero,'[1] said Narayani Ganesh, his daughter from Alamelu 'Bobji', his only legally recognized wife.

Gemini and Pushpavalli proved to be a successful on-screen pair and worked together in many films. More than their films, their affair was constantly talked about; at industry functions, on sets and at shoots, Pushpavalli would routinely be spotted with Gemini. He was, however, not ready to give this romance a formal name. Like Vasan, Gemini was already married (to Bobji).

An old story was playing out again in Pushpavalli's life. Through people close to her, rumours that Pushpavalli and Gemini had secretly got married in a temple made it to the tabloids and newspapers. However, no evidence ever surfaced to support these sensational reports. Pushpavalli tied her life down to Gemini. In her relationship with Vasan, she was the 'other woman'. In Gemini's life too, she played the same role. A role she had not wanted to accept and to avoid which she had left Vasan, and a promising career in Bombay.

In October 1954 their first daughter was born. She was named Bhanurekha.

5

Bhanurekha

'I was pulled out of the ninth class and made to work when I was 14... I was not to know how much in debt my mother was till much later... I used to refuse to go to the sets and occasionally my brother beat me up.' – Rekha

Bhanurekha's entry into the world was accompanied by gossip and rumour, and to be gossiped and whispered about remained her fate through life. Rumours of her being Gemini's illegitimate daughter spread like wildfire. She was told by her mother from early childhood that her name was Bhanurekha Ganesan, thus claiming for her daughter the legitimacy she always yearned for. The Ganesan name carried the dignity and respect that Pushpavalli desperately wanted. Dignity and respect, however, were rare commodities in the early 1950s for women who had children without being married.

~

Around the time Rekha was born, Gemini was shooting for the film *Manampol Mangalyam* (Marriage of Minds), which featured him in a double role. The actresses cast opposite him were Savithri and Surabhi Balasaraswathi. The film was hugely successful and became a milestone in Gemini's career. But in no time, rumours that he was having an affair with Savithri started swirling. These were closely followed by news of their wedding. Savithri and Gemini had secretly married at the Chamundi temple in Mysore. 'Theirs was a sustained union that lasted for more than a dozen years with a marriage, household and children. The Gemini-Savithri relationship worked wonders for their private as well as screen lives,' said Narayani Ganesh.

News of the wedding broke Pushpavalli's heart. Savithri had started using Ganesan as her surname. This was the one right that Gemini never gave Pushpavalli. Not even after begetting two daughters with her. Not even after she had devoted years and years of her life and career to him.

It is said that by the time their daughter Radha was born, when Rekha was around two years old, Pushpavalli and Gemini's relationship was on its last legs. Gemini had refused to accept them. He was now barely visiting their home. Slowly it came to a point where the children learnt more about their father through tabloids than through direct contact.

The deepest impact of this was felt by Bhanurekha, who, then in her formative years, was a keen and curious observer of the world. She knew her father was living in another house, where he had another family, one that he loved enormously, perhaps more than he loved her family. She knew he was a father only in name, one she could never really have all to herself.

Later, a dejected Pushpavalli got involved with another man, a cinematographer in the Madras film industry, K. Prakash.[1] She even started signing her name as K. Pushpavalli. They reportedly had two children together: a daughter, Dhanalakshmi, and a son, Seshu. In all, Pushpavalli had six children: Rekha and Radha with Gemini Ganesan and their half-siblings Babuji, Rama, Dhanalakshmi and Seshu.

It may have been easier for the children if they had had an anonymous, more ordinary father. But as Bhanurekha grew, so did her father's status in the film industry. He came to be known as one of the 'big three' of South Indian cinema of those times, along with M.G. Ramachandran and Sivaji Ganesan. Gemini's personal life was no secret. His 'illegitimate' children and the women in his life were ruthlessly exploited by gossip magazines. It became impossible for these associations to be pushed under the carpet.

Years later, Gemini himself termed his affairs illegal. He said in an interview, 'Savithri was not my wife. Nor were the other women in my life. I did introduce them as my wives in public, had children by them but all those were illegal relationships. I didn't commit bigamy legally.

I've just one wife, Bobji, the one I got married to when I was young.'

'Though he never lived with us, we "felt" his presence wherever we went, for whatever we did. My mother constantly spoke about him, his likes and dislikes. Whatever you wish to call it – love or affection – the feeling my mother had towards him was strong and positive that lasted throughout her life,' Rekha says in Narayani Ganesh's book *Eternal Romantic: My Father, Gemini Ganesan.*

Pushpavalli tried to make up for Gemini's absence and she and Bhanurekha grew close to each other. But Pushpavalli had to earn a living and spent much time shooting. Bhanurekha too worked in a film called *Rangula Ratnam* (1966) while still a pre-teen.

It was by the sound of the tiny bells on her anklets that the children would know Pushpavalli had returned home. 'Our love for our mother was almost like an obsession, the reason being that she was never in the house. Most of the time she was away for shooting. The day she stayed at home was like a festival. All of us wanted to sit on her lap. I resented her for the overpowering effect she had on us and for not being around when we needed her. But I was in awe of her all the same,'[2] Rekha recounted her childhood.

～

Gemini and Bobji's daughter, Narayani Ganesh, now a journalist, first met Bhanurekha at the Presentation Convent School, Madras. Remembering the encounter, Narayani wrote, 'A girl struck up conversation with me after school one day. I must have been nine or 10 years old. "Why do you and your sister go home in different cars?" she asked. I was puzzled. My two elder sisters had finished school and my younger sister was a baby. "Come, I will take you to her," she said holding my hand.' The two half-sisters met that day for the first time. 'She was pretty and her eyes were lined with mascara. She said her name was Bhanurekha. "What is your father's name," I asked. "Gemini Ganesan," pat came the reply. My eyes were filled with tears. How can that be? He was my father,'[3] she recalled. Later, Narayani also met Rekha's younger sister, Radha, and found her to be rather beautiful. According to her, Radha resembled her appa. At that young age, it was perhaps heart-breaking for her not to have exclusive rights over her father.

School must have been far more difficult for Bhanurekha and her sister than it was for Narayani. Bhanurekha saw the contempt in her classmates' eyes; they thought she was ugly, fat and 'illegitimate'. There were instances when she was mocked and called *lotta*, Tamil for bastard. Each day when attendance was taken, her name was called out: 'Bhanurekha Ganesan!' Each day she would come face-to-face with the lie she was forced to live. Her name evoked deep conflict within her. In such circumstances, bitterness can take root, spread and stay for a long time, perhaps forever.

~

Age was catching up with Pushpavalli. The film offers had dried up. And to top it all, she had acquired from Gemini a penchant for horse racing. Pushpavalli indulged in her hobby long after Gemini had exited her life. It became an addiction; she lost so much money at the races that she had to resort to borrowing more and more. To make matters worse, Pushpavalli went through a patch of ill health. She was at a dead end. Her eldest daughter, Rama, also kept ill health and her son Babuji, an aspiring composer, was struggling to find a foothold. Her other children were still in school.

The family was on the brink of collapse.

~

Then, on a fateful night in 1968, Bhanurekha, a young teenager, scribbled a suicide note: she had failed, again, in her exams and didn't want to live any more.

After hours of trying, the doctors were able to revive her. When she opened her eyes in the hospital, Pushpavalli, eyes brimming with tears, was right in front of her. Pushpavalli helped rebuild Bhanurekha's spirit.

They got talking, and she asked Bhanurekha what she wanted to do with her life. Pushpavalli offered to get her married. Or she could help Bhanurekha enter the film world, especially as she was being trained to be a dancer. There were three choices: films, studies or marriage.

Bhanurekha seemed ill-suited for the latter two paths, though the film world did not excite her much either. She had, after all, grown up exposed to the dark side of showbiz. But Bhanurekha's destiny, it seems, was preordained. She was to be the hope of Pushpavalli's crumbling household. Her reluctance notwithstanding, she was to become part of the cine-world. 'I was pulled out of the ninth class and made to work when I was 14. At that time it made no sense. I was the pampered child of the family, always given everything I wanted. It seemed to me that we were happy and certainly well-off. I was not to know how much in debt my mother was till much later. So the idea of working in films did not appeal to me at all. I used to refuse to go to the sets and occasionally my brother beat me up.'4

Pushpavalli was aware that though Gemini did not acknowledge it the entire Madras film fraternity knew Bhanurekha was his daughter. Gemini was not just a huge star in Tamil, Telugu and Kannada cinema but also a shrewd businessman and he had invested wisely in real estate and property development. But Bhanurekha enjoyed none of the benefits of being his daughter. Had he just made a phone call, there would have been a line of producers ready to sign up Bhanurekha. He had the stature and the financial power to launch his daughter's film career if he wanted. Instead, unaccepted by her father, Bhanurekha went, along with her mother, knocking on every producer's door for even a small role in a film.

At that time, cinema was viewed as a dishonourable profession for women. At fourteen, Bhanurekha understood this; she had to fight the lecherous looks that directors and producers gave her. While Bhanurekha battled the scorching heat as she waited outside studios in long queues for her turn to audition, her father's fans lined up outside other studios, waiting to catch a glimpse of him.

It has been speculated that many refused to give Bhanurekha work fearing Gemini's ire. However, the bigger and perhaps more decisive factor for Bhanurekha not getting work was that she did not *look* like a heroine. The odds were stacked against her.

Bhanurekha did manage to bag some small roles in Kannada and Tamil films. But finding work was difficult and the pay was meagre. Pushpavalli's hope was also showing signs of waning. She was coming to terms with the fact that her tomboyish daughter may not be typical heroine material. Maybe Bhanurekha wouldn't be able to achieve the success that Pushpavalli had enjoyed or fulfil her mother's dream of ruling over the Hindi film industry. But Pushpavalli was getting more desperate by the day and her loans were growing larger.

The Ganesan surname that Bhanurekha used wasn't

helping. To Bhanurekha, that name connoted a betrayal to her, and to her mother. Her surname was a lie. Her existence was based on a lie. Bhanurekha resolved not to live this lie any more. She wouldn't lead her life with this surname. She would find the respect her mother was denied. She would help her family and her mother. She could go to any lengths to give her mother the happiness that she deserved.

But first, this surname would have to exit her life.

6

Bollywood Debut

'Bombay was like a jungle, and I had walked in unarmed.
It was one of the most frightening phases of my life... Guys
did try and take advantage of my vulnerability.' – Rekha

The meagre earnings that Bhanurekha made as the second
lead in South Indian films was hardly enough to pay off
Pushpavalli's debt. So when it seemed that her daughter
might get signed by a Bombay-based film producer,
Pushpavalli was beside herself with happiness. Kuljeet
Pal had come looking for Bhanurekha after spotting her
in Gemini Studios at the end of 1968.

Kuljeet was a Nairobi-based businessman who had
come to Bombay to produce films. His second film,
Galiyon Ka Raja, had halted abruptly a few days into
the shooting because of a rift between the cast and the
director. The cast included Raaj Kumar, Mumtaz and
Hema Malini.

Dismayed by the starry tantrums, Kuljeet had gone to Madras to seek out the actor Biswajeet, who was shooting for *Paisa Ya Pyaar* (1969). Kuljeet was on the lookout for fresh faces for his next production, which was inspired by the English classic *King Solomon's Mines*. The Hindi version was to be named *Anjana Safar*.

Upon hearing the story, Biswajeet immediately agreed to be part of the project. Someone had recommended the southern heroine Vanisri for the female lead, and Kuljeet met her in the make-up room of a studio. But as they were talking, his eyes meandered over to a plump, dark-skinned girl sitting in a corner of the studio. Her plate was piled high with food, which she was eating hungrily.

The girl, he was told, was working as the second lead alongside Vanisri in the film. Someone let slip that she was the daughter of the veteran actress Pushpavalli. While talking to Vanisri, Kuljeet's eyes kept darting towards Bhanurekha. There was something unique about her innocence, her uninhibitedness, her spontaneity.

That very evening, Kuljeet was sitting in Pushpavalli's house. Moments later, Bhanurekha emerged from her room, draped in a Kanjeevaram sari, strange make-up lining her face.

Kuljeet asked her in English, 'Can you speak in Hindi?'
Pat came the reply, 'No.'

There was no way that Pushpavalli was going to lose this opportunity to make her daughter a film heroine. She intervened and said, 'My daughter's memory is very sharp. If you write down the lines for her, she can quickly memorize and deliver [them].' Kuljeet decided to test Pushpavalli's claim and dictated some lines in Hindi that Bhanurekha wrote down in the Roman script. She disappeared into her room to memorize the lines.

Barely had Kuljeet finished his cup of tea than Bhanurekha re-emerged from her room and confidently began spouting the lines that he had dictated in Hindi: *'Satish, ab toh woh din aa gaya hai jab tumhare aur mere beech mein ek phoolon ka haar bhi nahi hona chahiye. Humaare do jism aur do jaan ek hone chahiye.'* (Satish, the day has come when there should not be even a garland of flowers between you and me. Our bodies and souls should now be one.)

The lines were rather nonsensical, but Kuljeet couldn't believe that the Tamil-speaking girl had mastered them so convincingly. It was almost as if she was a native Hindi speaker.

'When I met this dark, plump girl who was playing a small role in a south film, I had an intuition that she would be a star. So, that very night, I met her mother Pushpavalli and signed her daughter on for a five-year contract,' Kuljeet said about his find. 'Her mother was very pleased when we came with her first Hindi offer. They were deep in debt. The mother kept asking for money saying, "the *Kabuliwala* is after me". Only later I realized she meant those Pathans who lend money at exorbitant rates.'[1]

Rekha recounted the same instance in these words: 'When I was offered Hindi films, my mother said that not only was it a chance of a lifetime, but that we needed the money. So I agreed.'[2]

The decision had been made. Thus began Bhanurekha's *anjana safar*, as her maiden Hindi film was aptly called, into the world of Hindi cinema.

~

In 1969, the fourteen-year-old Bhanurekha reached Bombay. The Hindi film industry was craving for change, in storylines, talent, fashion trends and faces. An older generation of stars was making way for a new one. The turning point came in 1969 when Rajesh Khanna's *Aradhana* became a blockbuster and over the next two years he eclipsed almost every other star with his dazzling successes. Actresses went from the 'natural look' of the 1950s and 1960s to a chicer, more tortuously coiffed and elaborately made-up look. Sharmila Tagore, Waheeda Rehman, Asha Parekh, Saira Banu and Mumtaz ruled the roost. Producers were forever on the lookout for new faces to tell fresh stories, and for lead actors for low-budget films.

It was also the year a tall, gawky man entered the film industry. He was ridiculed. The actor was launched by writer-film-maker Khwaja Ahmad Abbas in a small but significant role in his film *Saat Hindustani*. The film was a disaster at the box office. But the actor got a national award for his debut. His name was Amitabh Bachchan.

~

Bhanurekha's first home in Bombay was Room No. 115 in Hotel Ajanta in Juhu. She was to live there, all expenses paid, for the duration of the shooting of her debut film. Not just this, Kuljeet Pal's contract with her specified that she had to act in four films produced by him and another four by his brother, the director Shatrujeet Pal. For her first film, *Anjana Safar*, Bhanurekha was to be paid Rs 25,000, and for each successive film, the pay would be hiked by Rs 25,000. The Pals must have seen something in the tomboyish and naive Rekha, whose only talent at that time was to speak her mind and a photographic memory that helped her memorize dialogues in a language she didn't know. There were murmurs, and even published stories, which hinted that Rekha was being abused but there's no substantiation for this claim. The fact was that Bhanurekha had got a multiple-film offer.

Pushpavalli's happiness must have known no bounds. Her own unfulfilled dreams of making it big in the Bombay film industry were coming true for her daughter.

But, for Bhanurekha, things were anything but dreamy. Bombay was an alien city. It did not understand her restraint. It did not understand her need to be alone with herself. It did not understand her language. Time and again, she would feel angry at her mother who had pushed her there without knowing what she wanted. Little could console her and she convinced herself that things would get better once she began work.

'Bombay was like a jungle, and I had walked in unarmed. It was one of the most frightening phases of my life... I was totally ignorant of the ways of this new world. Guys did try and take advantage of my vulnerability. I did feel "What am I doing? I should be in school, having an ice-cream, fun with my friends, why am I even forced to work, deprived of normal things that a child should be doing at my age?" Every single day I cried, because I had to eat what I didn't like, wear crazy clothes with sequins and stuff poking into my body. Costume jewellery would give me an absolute terrible allergy. Hair spray wouldn't go off for days even despite all my washing. I was pushed, literally dragged from one studio to another. A terrible thing to do to a 13-year-old child,' she later recounted.[3]

Bhanurekha's reputation as the 'illegitimate' child of superstar Gemini Ganesan had followed her to Bombay. Her father was doing ten films a year, and had forayed into the Hindi film industry, starring opposite Meena Kumari, Vyjayanthimala, Kishore Kumar, etc. In her early days in Bombay itself, Bhanurekha realized that men were much the same everywhere, whether in Madras or in Bombay. In Madras at least Pushpavalli was a film industry veteran. In Bombay, without a godfather, the tender teenager was an easy target. Every seemingly benevolent gesture had the stench of ulterior motive. Every offer of a lead role came with strings attached. There was a price to be paid for being a girl that no one cared for, feared or respected. The writer and journalist Jerry Pinto, who has covered the Hindi film industry for years, said, Rekha 'could sketch out her journey from a child who came to Bollywood, who went through serial abuse at the hands of producers and film stars and directors, etc. Startling things where she talks about being a child and how people laughed at her.'[4] Such experiences are not easy to forget and can have a serious impact on a person's psyche.

~

In the film industry in India, the muhurat ceremony marks the commencement of the first shot of the film. The muhurat for Bhanurekha's first film, *Anjana Safar*, was held on 7 August 1969. The film was later renamed *Do Shikari*. People were in disbelief over producer Kuljeet's choice of heroine. Kuljeet recalled, 'Raaj Kumar told me, "You're from Africa. No wonder you like black girls!"'[5] Within days, however, the girl he discovered in Madras would go on to sign many more films.

Pushpavalli's daughter defied the conventional heroine mould and broke many Bollywood stereotypes. She was dark-skinned, had a 33-inch waist[6] and didn't speak any Hindi. She blindly took all the roles that came her way and remained undeterred by gossip and criticism. 'I was called the "Ugly Duckling" of Hindi films because of my dark complexion and south Indian features. I used to feel deeply hurt when people compared me with the leading heroines of the time and said I was no match for them. I was determined to make it big.'[7]

Her strong willpower paid off and within a week the muhurat of Kuljeet's brother Shatrujeet's first film, *Mehmaan*, starring Bhanurekha, was held in Bombay. Then, on 20 August, the film *Haseenon Ka Devta*, produced by Ram Dayal, was launched, in which she starred opposite Sanjay Khan. On 30 August, Mohan Sehgal's *Sawan Bhadon* went on the floors.

Only a month old in Bombay and she had four films in hand. The fourteen-year-old Bhanurekha had single-handedly turned around the fortunes of her family. Then she changed her own. The new city and a new life also came with a new name for Bhanurekha Ganesan, a name without a surname. All her films had the same name in the credit roll for lead actress: Rekha.

7

The Kiss of 'Life'

'I didn't do it. I was taken by surprise. Nothing could've compensated, nothing can wipe off what I felt. Not even the coverage it got in Life *magazine.'* – Rekha[1]

It is rather strange and hypocritical that while Indian cinema has always banked on raunchy dances, dialogues thick with double entendre and extreme violence to gain audiences, kissing scenes between an actor and actress have remained taboo. Barring a few exceptions, most film-makers and artists avoid such scenes. If the plot does build up to a kiss, in place of the climax, the camera pans away to focus on flowers, sunsets, waterfalls and other such banalities. This cloak of cinematic hypocrisy would be shed only when the pressures of success pushed producers and stars to sensational publicity stunts. Kuljeet Pal and Biswajeet were looking for such a sensational publicity stunt.

The shooting of *Anjana Safar* was under way in Bombay's Mahboob Studio. Raja Nawathe was the director and cinematographer of the film. In the very first schedule of the film, Kuljeet, Raja and Biswajeet had hatched a plan, with Rekha as the unsuspecting victim.

That day a romantic scene was to be filmed between Rekha and Biswajeet. Every last detail of the strategy had been decided before the shoot, and the camera was set to record each moment. As soon as the director Raj Nawathe said 'action', Biswajeet took Rekha in his arms and pressed his lips on hers. Rekha was stunned. This kiss had never been mentioned to her. The camera kept rolling; neither was the director ordering 'cut' nor was Biswajeet letting go of her. For all of five minutes, Biswajeet kept kissing Rekha. Unit members were whistling and cheering. Those voices were said to have echoed in Rekha's conscience till much later. Her eyes were tightly shut but they were full of tears.

Recalling the day, Biswajeet referred to the incident as Raja Nawathe's idea. Raja had insisted that he kiss Rekha, not yet fifteen, catching her by surprise. Biswajeet maintained that it was not his fault, that he was merely working on the director's instructions. 'It was not for my enjoyment, but important for the film. Rekha felt betrayed and was furious,' admitted Biswajeet.[2]

Rekha felt betrayed, cheated and exploited by what had happened. But she couldn't say a word in protest. She knew that the consequences of creating a scene would be dire: she would be thrown out of the film. Her end would have begun before her beginning.

True to filmi cliché, her silence was taken to be her assent. News spread like wildfire in the industry that there was a new South Indian actress in town who did not shy away from 'bold' scenes. Kuljeet Pal is said to have fed more salacious information on Rekha's life to film magazines. Not a single one of her films was ready but the image of being 'bold' was foisted on her. She was called a 'sex kitten'. A fourteen-year-old 'sex kitten'.

But there was another side to the story. In an interview later, Kuljeet Pal would claim that Rekha was present when he decided there would be a kissing scene between Biswajeet and her. 'Rekha was there. She said that she has no reservations against a kissing scene. She said she would do it. I know she now says that she was taken by surprise when Biswajeet kissed her. I only told her that since she is doing something which Hindi film heroines don't, it will be better if she said she absolutely did not like it. But she knew about this scene in all cases.'[3]

We'll never know the truth. But Rekha would now be known as the diva who did not shy away from using her sexuality to her advantage. Was she really the victim here?

Jerry Pinto has firm opinions on the exploitation common in the Bombay film industry: 'I think many of these actresses were abused as children. Neetu Singh, Rekha, all these triumphant divas.' Pinto avers that even Waheeda Rehman was abused by Guru Dutt. 'And she

[Waheeda Rehman] was sixteen or something so she was technically a minor…even if it was consensual, it was abuse. It makes you pause because you think so highly of Guru Dutt. These are things that can scar you. And I think Rekha was definitely scarred,' Pinto asserted.[4]

Rekha was being projected as a cunning and conniving actor; it was said that she did what she did for publicity. But it cannot be denied that she was fourteen at the time of the incident. And the only person willing to speak up for her was herself. Sometimes she denied, sometimes she accepted complicity in the kiss.

~

On 28 March 1968, the Government of India had constituted an inquiry committee on the issue of film censorship. The committee was responsible for setting down rules and guidelines for kissing and sex scenes in films. Retired chief justice of the Punjab High Court G.D. Khosla was the chairman of the committee. Members of the committee included R.K. Narayan, Khwaja Ahmad Abbas, Balraj Sahni and Nargis. The Khosla committee submitted its report to the government in 1969.

The recommendations of the report, considered bold for its times, said, 'If, in telling the story, it is logical, relevant or necessary to depict a passionate kiss or a nude human figure, there should be no question of excluding the shot, provided the theme is handled with delicacy and feeling, aiming at aesthetic expression and avoiding all suggestion of prurience or lasciviousness.'

The Khosla committee report won accolades for its progressive take on the issue, though in later years it would be completely ignored by successive governments. The Supreme Court praised the recommendations, and the report sparked a debate on censorship. The noise that thus ensued could be heard far and wide; in 1969 the cover story of the Asia edition of the famous international magazine *Life* was titled 'India's Kissing Crisis: To Kiss or Not To...'

James Shepherd, the American journalist who came to India to cover the issue, wanted to interview an actress who would be willing to get photographed kissing for the story. While doing his research, he met Randhir Kapoor in R.K. Studio. Randhir was busy directing his first film, *Kal, Aaj Aur Kal* (1971), in which he also made his debut as a lead actor. He told James about Rekha, and how the scandalous kissing scene was still being talked about in the industry. The American journalist decided to talk to her.

News that *Life* was planning a cover story reached Rekha too. She knew that *Life* was a reputed and credible magazine, and saw this as a platform to contribute to the debate. This was also a golden opportunity to convert the negative publicity from the kissing episode into positive coverage. Being covered by *Life* could boost her career no end, and Rekha agreed to feature in its story. *Life* published two photographs of Biswajeet and Rekha kissing. One was a still from *Anjana Safar* and the other was taken especially for the magazine story. The report also carried photographs of Simi Garewal and Persis Khambatta, but Rekha's photographs got all the attention. None of Rekha's films had as yet released but she had already been featured in an international magazine. Thanks to these two pictures, her reputation as the industry 'sex symbol' solidified.

~

To get maximum mileage out of the buzz around the *Life* magazine cover, Kuljeet Pal organized a press conference, Rekha's first, at the Shalimar hotel in Bombay. Rekha would have to face a group of film scribes hungry for 'sexy' quotes from a bold new starlet who didn't shy away from kissing on screen.

They asked Rekha, 'So you are in favour of kissing?'

'Yes,' answered Rekha.

'In which situations?' asked the scribe.

'When the heroine is wearing slacks.'

It's difficult to say if this was a stupid answer or a tongue-in-cheek statement but it confused the media. Rekha kept smiling.

'Why have you come to Hindi films?' one of them asked.

'Because they don't pay much in Tamil, Telugu and Malayalam films...'

They laughed at her childlike and honest answers. There

was no one like Rekha that the press had seen before. So young, so confident, so blunt and so naive. It was a heady mix. The media lapped it all up.

~

The kiss got national and international attention, a fabulous start for any debutante in show business. Although no A-list actress of that time commented on the kiss, everyone had become aware of Rekha's entry into the film world.

For Rekha, the lessons were learnt and firmly ingrained: every scandal is publicity, every tragedy an opportunity.

8

'Madrasan'

'How is this dark, plump and gauche actress ever going to make it?' – Shashi Kapoor

The months passed by quickly. Rekha was surrounded by much hype though none of her films were anywhere near completion. That's when she resorted to advertisements to earn some extra money. Two of her ad films were directed by Shyam Benegal, a known name in advertising at that time. He shot Rekha in an advertisement for Gold Spot, the soft drink. Remembering Rekha and those ad films makes his eyes sparkle. Benegal recalls, 'She was very young, must be fourteen or fifteen. But what I noticed about her, from the time I made that ad film, was the incredible confidence she always had in front of the camera; her presence was always very confident and vivacious. She was very attractive in a different sort of way but she had yet to flower.'[1] Rekha didn't really conform with the image of a stereotypical film actress, and she couldn't converse well in Hindi. Still, the teenager's tremendous self-confidence touched Benegal's heart. Years later, when he became an acclaimed film-maker, he directed Rekha as the lead in *Kalyug* (1981), considered among the best films of her career.

~

Just when Rekha had come to Bombay, the producer-director Mohan Sehgal was looking for a new heroine for his film *Sawan Bhadon*. He needed a heroine who could essay the role of a village belle. Though he had signed a Bombay actress, Jayshree T., for the film, he did not think she was best suited for the role.

In Rekha, Sehgal found the childlike innocence he wanted in his heroine. He called Rekha and Pushpavalli for a meeting but Rekha was reluctant to meet Sehgal; she didn't want to sign any more films and go through the ritual of producers 'observing' her to decide whether she could work for their film. When her mother insisted, she was furious but still accompanied her for the meeting. Sehgal could sense that Rekha was upset. Her monosyllabic replies to all his questions was no.

'Will you work in my film?'

'No.'

'Do you know Hindi?'

'No.'

'If I train you as an actor and give you good clothes, still no?'

'No.'

'No! Is this the dialogue you want to speak in my film?'

Sehgal was clearly irritated. Rekha's eyes were glued to the ground but her lips curved into a slight smile.

Sehgal looked at Pushpavalli and said, 'She is the heroine of my film.' Rekha's mother heaved a sigh of relief and said, 'Baby will do it. I promise you.'

Sehgal had already chosen a hero for *Sawan Bhadon*: the new actor Navin Nischol. A tall and dapper Punjabi, Nischol had recently finished training as an actor at the prestigious Film and Television Institute of India at Pune, where he had won a gold medal. Though this was only his first film, he threw temper tantrums, perhaps owing partially to his gold medal and a bit to the heady feeling of signing a film. As soon as he got to know that Sehgal had signed Rekha for the film, he remarked, 'Mohanji, from where did you pick out this *namoona* [character]? *Itni kaali-kalooti* [So dark and ugly]!'[2]

Nischol's remark made it to the gossip columns and Rekha became the butt of several industry jokes. Thanks to his audacious statement, and the traction that it got, Nischol's later interviews were published widely in many magazines. Rekha and he were pitted against each other by the press. Comparisons were drawn between the two, with some saying it was a mistake to cast a heroine like

Rekha opposite a gold-medallist actor and that Nischol's career was being trifled with.

Sehgal was only too happy with all the petty sniping that was getting his film more publicity. He had decided that come what may Rekha would remain the heroine of his film. She fit the role of the village damsel Chanda rather well. Jayshree T. was given the role of the modern city girl Dolly, Nischol's sister in the movie, and the actresses became good friends. Jayshree T. shares, 'In those days, she [Rekha] had that honest quality about her. We became friends. I felt she had a complex about her complexion. She was very raw but very cheerful. Like South Indians speak Hindi, she used to shout: *"Ae kidhar thi tu!"'* (Hey, where were you!)

~

Sawan Bhadon went on the floors on 11 October 1969. But Rekha got an unpleasant surprise on the very first day of shooting. Though her hair was quite long and thick, she was made to wear a wig; in those days it was trendy for heroines to wear hairpieces in films. But the wig wouldn't sit well atop Rekha's voluminous hair. Frustrated, the hairdressers Khatoon and Khateeja drastically cut Rekha's hair, much to her anguish.

But that wasn't all. In front of the fair Nischol, Rekha appeared dark. Such a heroine was considered unacceptable. 'I was standing for an hour while someone body-painted me from head to toe. Because in those days, heroines were required to be fair. In the north they have this fairness hang-up. They painted all the junior artists white in all of D. Ramanaidu films,'[3] Rekha said.

Remembering those days, Jayshree T. says, 'At that time, Rekha had no clue about make-up. She totally depended on make-up persons who had no clue what to do with her heavy face. She had no idea about bleaching and waxing. She would come to my room and see me applying eyeliner. She was very lonely and we became good friends. Till date we address each other as Chanda and Dolly, the names of our characters in *Sawan Bhadon*.'

According to a unit member of *Sawan Bhadon*, the crew would not think twice before making Rekha the butt of cruel jokes. She was the only South Indian among Punjabi-, Hindi- and Marathi-speakers. Unable to speak these languages, Rekha couldn't understand their jibes. But their tone and gestures left no doubt that the barbs were directed at Rekha. 'They like to believe it was funny. But I didn't think it was funny,'[4] Rekha said, recollecting how the unit members made fun of her in Hindi.

Undeterred, Rekha would diligently memorize her lines in Hindi. Sehgal used to guide her in correct diction and intonation.

The 'Madrasan' Rekha, working with a unit full of North Indians, felt lonely in the silence of Room No. 115 at Hotel Ajanta at night, and even through the din of shooting during the day.

Since childhood, loneliness had been her closest companion.

~

As the shooting of *Sawan Bhadon* progressed, Sehgal was convinced that signing Rekha had not been a mistake. A strange energy would enliven her as soon as the camera started rolling, the same kind of energy that was the hallmark of the actress Mumtaz. Rekha's dialogue delivery was so good that no one could guess that she did not know Hindi; she remembered each and every word of her lines. Nischol later said that his first impression of Rekha quickly changed as she revealed herself to be a 'boisterous tomboy' and they quickly became buddies.

Sawan Bhadon had Rekha playing a feisty village girl, Chanda, who saves the London-educated rich boy Vikram (Navin Nischol) from local hitmen out to kill him. Chanda and her friends do that by breaking earthen water pots over their heads! And, like it happens in Hindi films of the 1970s, the polished, suave Vikram immediately falls in love with the rustic Chanda.

Sawan Bhadon was a run-of-the-mill film that will also be remembered for its large assortment of wigs and the beehive hairdos of the lead actors. Almost everyone in the film, including Navin Nischol and, of course, Rekha, wore outlandish wigs. Rekha's costumes were garish. 'If you look at *Sawan Bhadon*, she is pink up to her chin and brown

on her neck. Her clothes don't fit her. She has pimples,'
says Jerry Pinto.

But Rekha brought a lot of spunk and charm to her
character with her confidence and raw comic timing. Most
of the film's reviews criticized her waistline and costumes
but praised her confidence.

Sonik–Omi composed some masala chartbusters that
were a sure-shot way to ensure that the film was talked
about. '*Kaan mein jhumka*' was among the top songs of
the year.

~

The premiere of *Sawan Bhadon* was held at Bombay's
Novelty Cinema in September 1970. The guests were
shocked when they caught sight of the film's debutante
heroine, a dusky, plump fifteen-year-old whose 33-inch
waist strained against her gaudy black-and-blue sequined
gharara. A bouffant with stiff kiss curls and a profusion of
ringlets completed the picture. An amazed Shashi Kapoor
uttered in disbelief, 'How is this dark, plump and gauche
actress ever going to make it?'[5]

His wife, Jennifer, however, recognized the inexplicable
star quality of the teenager and prophesied that she would
become the darling of the people in the years to come.
Jennifer's prophecy was to come magnificently true.

Sawan Bhadon was a thumping success and celebrated
silver jubilees everywhere. It was a non-star-cast, low-

budget movie that broke the stranglehold over the box office of productions with big stars. And it propelled two newcomers to stardom's dizzy heights. Both Nischol and Rekha signed up movies by the dozen.

A party was thrown to introduce Rekha to the press. Most newcomers are shy and hesitant, but not Rekha; she was outspoken and bold when answering questions from the press. She was never at a loss for a quick comeback, and by the end of the party it was clear that she had completely won over the journalists. They had never encountered anyone, young or old, who was as frank and fearless as this brash, young girl. She became a lot more confident after the success of her films.

Rekha had nothing to lose. She had risen from the bottom, both personally and professionally. This was a tremendous experience for a fifteen-year-old. There were those who wondered whether Rekha had been coached to make provocative statements. Yes, perhaps life had been a good coach.

~

The year 1970 also saw the emergence of two other important actresses of Hindi cinema. Though Hema Malini had already made her debut opposite Raj Kapoor in 1968 with *Sapno Ka Saudagar*, 1970 saw the release of five of her films. *Johny Mera Naam* opposite Dev Anand went on to become the biggest blockbuster of the year. The film remained the most successful of Dev Anand's illustrious career and catapulted the lead actress to stardom.

The other actress was cast by the film-maker Hrishikesh Mukherjee straight out of the Film and Television Institute of India. The actress, like Nischol, had won a gold medal in the acting course. She was Jaya Bhaduri, the eldest daughter of Taroon Kumar Bhaduri, a writer, journalist and stage artist in Bhopal.

Unlike Rekha's debut in a mainstream masala film, Mukherjee had launched Jaya in *Guddi*, in which she played a strong central character, a fourteen-year-old obsessed with the film star Dharmendra. The film was a success and Jaya was hailed as the next big thing and a *serious actress* to look out for. The image stuck for the rest of her career.

Rekha, on the other hand, wasn't really thought of as an 'actress' at all. But she was busy signing formula films left, right and centre.

9

Vin Vin and Kin Kin

'I am not just an actress, but I am a badnaam *actress with a rotten past and a reputation for being a sex maniac.'* – Rekha

Rekha very quickly became popular in the industry. At one point, there were about twenty-five Rekha-starrers on the floors. She was doing double shifts, though none of her films were much to write home about. Her potboilers like *Saaz Aur Sanam* (1971) with Premendra, *Haseenon Ka Devta* (1971) with Sanjay Khan and *Elaan* (1971) with Vinod Khanna and Vinod Mehra came and went.

However, Rekha made sure that her interviews kept her in the news. She told one interviewer, 'You can't come close, really close, to a man without making love.'[1] And that 'It is sheer fluke that I have never got pregnant so far.'[2] She also boldly approved of 'free love',[3] a euphemism for premarital sex in those times. Perhaps she didn't realize that such interviews gave her an image that would be difficult to shed.

For his film *Ek Bechara* (1972), the producer B.N. Ghosh signed Rekha in 1971 as the heroine alongside Jeetendra, her first A-list co-star, popularly known as 'Jumping Jack'. Jeetendra had amassed a huge female following after the success of his film *Farz* (1967). Also, and importantly, he was still unmarried. Having watched many of his films, Rekha was somewhat smitten with this handsome, young Punjabi actor. It was reported that Jeetendra soon became her friend.

The first shoot for the film was organized in Shimla and it did not take long for reports of a steaming romance between Jeetendra and Rekha to waft out of the cold mountains. According to reports from the shoot, Jeetendra encouraged the closeness. Rekha had, till then, mostly faced jeers and mockery from the industry. This was the first time, perhaps, that she felt loved and respected. Jeetendra brought a sparkle to Rekha's eyes. The romance continued once the young couple was back in Bombay. They went on long drives and for romantic dinners. Rekha, as usual, didn't hold back and openly talked about their closeness.

Despite her casual attitude towards acting as a profession and a total lack of discipline, especially when she was in love, some of Rekha's films tasted success. That her costumes were especially designed keeping in mind her décolletage must have helped. After the success of *Ek*

Bechara, Rekha and Jeetendra signed another film together, *Anokhi Ada* (1973). It was widely published that Rekha's mother, too, was very fond of Jeetendra.

But, like all Bollywood love stories, this one also had a twist. Jeetendra had a long-standing girlfriend, Shobha, who worked as an air hostess. This became the cause of many altercations between Rekha and him, but Jeetendra was just not ready to leave Shobha. After much heartache and suffering, it dawned on Rekha that the relationship was nothing more than 'time pass' for Jeetendra.

The cracks in their relationship were exposed to the public during the shooting of *Anokhi Ada*. Rekha and Jeetendra were prone to brawling in front of others. Then, one day on the film sets, with several junior artistes present, Jeetendra said something to his hangers-on that revealed his true opinion about Rekha. Rekha overheard him and, her eyes welling up with tears, she ran to her make-up room and burst out crying.

Following this, all conversation between Rekha and Jeetendra came to a halt. *Anokhi Ada* was completed with utmost difficulty. The tension between the two lead actors was evident: the post-interval love scenes in the film were just put-ons for the benefit of the cameras. When the cameras went off, Rekha and Jeetendra avoided each other's eyes, pretending to be total strangers.

Later in an interview, Rekha recalled those days with immense bitterness: 'I hate the man who destroyed my childhood ideals of love, romance and marriage. There was a time when I was like other girls too. I only wanted one guy of my own to look up to, to adore, to trust. And I trusted Jeetu. I didn't hanker after marriage or anything at that time. I only wanted him to be fair to me, to give as much as he got out of this relationship.'[4]

~

In 1971 Vinod Mehra began his career as the hero in *Ek Thi Rita*. He had worked in several films as a child artist, including *Raagini* (1958), in which he played Kishore Kumar's childhood self, *Angulimaal* (1960) and a small role in I.S. Johar's *Bewakoof* (1960).

Honest, warm and full of verve, Vinod met Rekha at a time she was trying to rebuild herself after being heartbroken by Jeetendra. Vinod himself was trying to find a foothold in the industry, unaware of how cruel it could be to newcomers. They began meeting each other and grew close. Rekha endearingly called him Vin Vin. Soon, it was said, neither could live without the other.

A gentleman to the fingertips, Vinod seems to have been the first genuine lover to come into Rekha's life. They were seen together everywhere, holding hands, kissing, driving around in Vinod's Volkswagen, having dinner in the wee hours of the morning in a cosy corner of the Taj restaurant, Shamiana. The director Saawan Kumar used to live in the flat adjacent to Vinod's in a building called Nibbana on Pali Hill. He says Rekha spent most of her time with Vinod, which was how he met her. Saawan went on to cast Rekha in five of his films, the most she has made with any director. Vinod and Rekha were so close that she was the unofficial hostess at Vinod's sister's wedding – and that says a lot.

Rekha was not one to hush up the relationship or hide her growing fondness for Vinod. In a 1972 interview with *Star and Style*, she said, 'Vinod kissed me on my birthday but in the morning and in the privacy of my bedroom.'

~

Whenever Rekha came under fire from the media, Vinod was at hand to defend her. People close to Rekha say that he was the first man to sincerely love her for who she was. Despite her audacious statements and colourful past, he wanted to give their relationship a name.

All was going well, but there was one hitch: Kamla Mehra, Vinod's mother.

Like a typical filmi mother-in-law, Kamla wanted her daughter-in-law to be docile, traditional and cultured. Rekha's image, in her eyes, was exactly the opposite of an ideal daughter-in-law's. Her bold disposition and sensational statements, often about premarital sex and her desire to become a mother, even if out of wedlock, did not go down well with Vinod's mother. 'Premarital sex is very natural. And all those prudes who say that a single woman should have sex only on her *suhaag raat* are talking bull,'[5] said Rekha in one interview.

Rekha's biggest disqualifier, however, was that she was born of a relationship that had no acceptance in society. Kamla Mehra had resolved that under no circumstances would her son marry this woman.

At Vinod's prodding, Rekha tried her best to be amicable with his mother and develop good relations with her. She would go to Nibbana to spend time with his sister Sharda and also prepare fish curry for 'Mummy'. As time went by, however, the futility of her efforts became obvious. Vinod tried hard to bridge the chasm between his mother and Rekha, but the latter's past, her bold film scenes and carefree statements proved to be an insurmountable roadblock.

Vinod also wanted Rekha to change and this became a bone of contention between them, often leading to full-blown arguments. Rekha started fearing that Vinod would desert her and in mid 1973, after one such altercation, she swallowed the cockroach poison Tik-20. Whiff of this tragedy reached the media in no time, and chaos, commotion and controversy followed. Many producers who had signed Rekha for their films made a beeline for Pushpavalli.

To contain matters, Rekha and Vinod hastily called for a press conference, to state that Rekha had not attempted suicide. This was a case of mere food poisoning, they claimed. The naive cover-up fed to the press was that Rekha had eaten some upma into which a cockroach had accidentally fallen. Naturally, this became the subject of industry ridicule and joke. 'To her [Vinod Mehra's mother] I am not just an actress, but I am a *badnaam* actress with a rotten past and a reputation for being a sex-maniac. For Vinod's sake she tolerated me in the beginning. Now she won't tolerate me at all,' Rekha said in an interview in September 1973.[6]

Perhaps as a result of the extreme step that Rekha had taken, Vinod agreed to get married. But it was decided that until the wedding ceremony was over, Vinod's mother would not be told. She would be amicably persuaded, and presented with a fait accompli, after the wedding. Preparations for the wedding were made by Babu (Ritesh Chatterjee), Moushumi Chatterjee's husband. The wedding was to be solemnized in a temple in Calcutta's Park Circus area and, touchingly, Moushumi gave Rekha her nose pin to wear.

Rekha was not overly bothered with the fact that married heroines seldom had a future in the film industry and that her marriage to Vinod could prove fatal for her career. She was aglow with the prospect of getting married and being accepted, socially and personally, in a dignified relationship. She was apparently happy and content, and had great hopes of marital bliss.

After getting married in Calcutta, Vinod and Rekha

returned to Bombay, and drove straight to Nibbana from the airport. But a storm was waiting to assail them there.

The incident was gossiped about in the industry for long after, finding its way into masala columns of film magazines. Here's what happened that day at the Mehra residence according to a film-maker:

As soon as the new bride bent to touch her mother-in-law's feet, Kamla Mehra angrily pushed her away. She refused to let Rekha enter her house. She lost her cool and abused and humiliated Rekha, who was standing at the front door. Vinod tried to intervene but Kamla was livid, so angry that at one point she took off her chappal and almost beat up Rekha with it. The poor girl was numb and confused. A crowd started to gather around the flat, and Rekha, stunned, hurt and shook up, started to run towards the lift, her eyes burning with tears. Vinod followed and told her to stay at her house till his mother calmed down.

With shock and hurt in her eyes, she agreed. Kamla Mehra's harsh words must have been reverberating in her ears.

A few months were spent trying to get Kamla to come around, during which time Rekha stayed at her own house. Vinod, stuck between his mother and wife, wasn't able to act decisively.

Rekha and Vinod's marriage was the hottest topic of discussion for industry insiders and film magazines.

However, in 2004, Rekha flatly denied ever having married Vinod Mehra.[7] She said Vinod was only a close friend.

~

In 1972 and 1973, sixteen films featuring Rekha were released, a staggering number by any standard. The only notable film, however, was *Rampur Ka Lakshman* (1972), with the hit song '*Gum Hai Kisi Ke Pyaar Mein*'. The success of the crime thrillers *Keemat* (1973) and *Kahani Kismat Ki* (1973) signalled to producers that the Rekha–Dharmendra pairing was commercially successful; in the years to come it would be fully exploited by many film-makers. *Keemat* also had a famous below-the-shower-in-a-towel song sequence featuring Rekha.

Rekha was also seen in Hrishikesh Mukherjee's *Namak Haraam* (1973), starring the reigning superstar, Rajesh Khanna, and the upcoming star Amitabh Bachchan. This was her first film with Amitabh but they had no scenes together.

Despite working in an astounding number of films, Rekha wasn't talked about for her acting. What kept her in magazine cover stories were her affairs and legendary indiscipline.

~

Kiran Kumar, the son of the famous Bollywood villain Jeevan, started his career with Khwaja Ahmad Abbas's *Do Boond Paani* (1971) after graduating from the Film and Television Institute of India. Though the film won several awards, Kiran went on to work in a number of B-grade films like *Jungle Mein Mangal* (1972), *Free Love* (1974) and *Gaal Gulaabi Nain Sharaabi* (1974). Neither the films nor Kiran clicked.

Kiran dated Rekha's close friend Yogita Bali for two years between 1972 and 1974. Rekha used to be Yogita's agony aunt. 'She [Rekha] was overprotective, and I became totally dependent on her,'[8] Yogita said about her bond with Rekha. She would often ask Rekha for advice. Little did she know that Rekha would herself cause her much agony. 'I think that was the first crack in our friendship. Initially, Kiran considered her a bad influence on me, and told me I should stop seeing her,' shares Yogita, who was hardly prepared for what was about to happen. Then rumours starting floating about an affair between Kiran and Rekha. Yogita was mature enough to realize that it takes two hands to clap; it would be unfair to blame only the woman: 'If they came together, Kiran must have been equally responsible. His seeing so much of Rekha definitely broke up our affair.'

A new man had entered Rekha's life and she lovingly called him Kin Kin. Rekha and Kiran started appearing together at film parties. Kiran took to frequenting Rekha's sets, and she would often vanish from shoots to spend time at Kiran's plush bungalow 'Jeevan Kiran' in Bandra, built by his father. Rekha, as usual, liberally shared details of her relationship with Kiran, and they made their way into film magazines.

~

When Rekha was involved with Vinod Mehra, not a week passed without producers complaining of her errant behaviour during shoots. She routinely played truant to be with Vinod, which caused huge financial losses to her producers. This trend continued during her relationship with Kiran Kumar.

Once she was shooting in Mahabaleshwar for Feroz Khan's *Dharmatma* (1975). After one shot, there was a short break for the lights to be moved about for the next scene. When everything was ready, Feroz Khan sent for Rekha. But she was nowhere to be found. Someone told him that she had driven off in her car. For two days there was no sign of Rekha. When she finally returned, she said that she had driven all the way to Bombay on a whim, because she was missing Kin Kin.

Ace cameraman of those times, N. Sriniwas remembers waiting for her for hours at some shoots: 'There are some stars who can never change. Like Raaj Kumar and Rekha. If a producer signs them on, it means he is mentally prepared for a long delay.'

Nothing else mattered to Rekha if she was in love. The producer Shiv Kumar, who signed Rekha for his film, narrated a bitter experience. A shoot had been arranged in Calcutta and Rekha arrived late for it. At the airport, she asked the man who had been sent to receive her, 'Where is everyone else?' The man said the whole unit was waiting on location. Upon getting there, Rekha found them playing cards. She immediately went to the producer and said, 'Since you people aren't doing any work I might as well go back to Bombay.'[9]

The producer protested, saying that they had been waiting only for her, and that it was only now that they could start work. But Rekha was unmoved: 'It's Kiran's birthday tomorrow. I must be with him. If I leave immediately I'll just be able to catch my flight to Bombay.' Finally, Shiv Kumar got her to promise that she would return in two days. She never came back at all.

Rekha in love was a dangerous person. Or so it was widely thought. Impulsive, irresponsible, reckless. No one thought she would ever change.

~

Kiran's father, Jeevan, a Kashmiri Pandit who had been working in the film industry for decades, soon learnt of their relationship. Being an industry veteran, he got to hear much about Rekha; industry folks frequently alluded to her scandalous past and present. Rekha was doggedly pursued by malicious gossip about her being promiscuous, and Jeevan was convinced that such a woman could not become a part of his family. The 'illegitimacy' of her birth was also frequently brought up. Kiran's family decisively turned Rekha down. But what must have hurt more was that Kiran, like Vinod Mehra earlier, didn't take a stand for her. Once more, Rekha had given her all only to be heartbroken again.

People close to Rekha in those days say that while the affairs were portrayed as casual flings by the media, Rekha gave her soul to each relationship. They consumed her completely and made her lose sight of her work and career. In her relationships with both Vinod Mehra and Kiran Kumar, she had to face rejection not because the couple had issues, but because society did. The shallow morals of society were dictating the course of her life, repeatedly robbing her of happiness.

~

Till then, Rekha had not been offered a film that could potentially establish her as a *serious actress*. But her hold on the industry was such that no issue of a film magazine was complete without mention of her. Being a media favourite was an art she excelled in and it played an important role in her career. Commenting on this, the senior film journalist Bhawana Somaaya said that Rekha was very open and friendly with the press: 'Rekha was a journalist's delight. She gave scoops, she made bold statements, she made for interesting write-ups – swallowing Tik-20 and committing suicide or eloping to marry Vinod Mehra. They knew exactly when the Vin Vin chapter ended and when the Kin Kin story started. She made confidential observations like, "it's sheer fluke that I've not got pregnant so far, though I wouldn't mind having a baby without marriage – I love kids".'[10]

10

Didibhai

'The fact that he was a married man doesn't make any kind of a difference. A rose is a rose is a rose.' – Rekha

After the success of her first few films, Rekha bought her own flat in Bombay in 1972. Leaving Hotel Ajanta, she shifted to Juhu's Beach Apartments at age eighteen. In the same apartment building lived the actress Jaya Bhaduri, who had by then firmly established herself as an actress par excellence. She had the range to easily fit the needs of commercial as well as 'meaningful' cinema. This was why she was counted amongst the most versatile, important and serious actors of that time.

Rekha and Jaya began their film careers around the same time. Their growth trajectories as actors, however, were starkly different. Neither did Rekha take herself seriously as an actress nor did the industry. The chatter surrounding her wasn't about her work; rather it was her personal life and sundry proclivities that hogged the limelight. 'I treat work as if it is fun. I bunk shooting like girls bunk college. Only they pay money to the colleges. In my case, producers pay me money… I was daring but I was also petrified of those producers tracing me…hunting for me…phoning me. I would hide at a friend's place and next day pretend to be sick on the sets.'[1] Whether it was Sunil Dutt or the reigning superstar of that time, Rajesh Khanna, Rekha had the gumption to keep everyone waiting. Once even Hrishikesh Mukherjee had to abandon a shoot on a set of *Namak Haraam* (1973) because, despite waiting for half a day, Rekha never showed up. Rekha was still a teenager at that time. She was known to be emotional, sensitive and free-spirited.

~

At Beach Apartments, Rekha and Jaya would often meet. Rekha affectionately called Jaya 'Didibhai', and frequently went over to Jaya's flat to spend time with her. The latter would advise her on life and career. It was there that Rekha first met Jaya's boyfriend, Amitabh Bachchan.

The son of the famous Hindi poet and writer Harivansh Rai Bachchan, Amitabh started his career with Khwaja Ahmad Abbas's *Saat Hindustani* (1969). The film was a flop and so were most of the subsequent films in which he played the lead. In fact, so bad was his luck that after being signed for a film with Rekha called *Duniya Ka*

Mela (1974), and even though shooting had started, he was replaced with Sanjay Khan by the producer G.M. Roshan, who was convinced that Amitabh was jinxed. Amitabh and Rekha, though, had already shot the song '*Tauba Tauba*' – their first one together, it is available on YouTube – for the film, but the two did not get to interact much.

It is said that during those times Amitabh's girlfriend Jaya was a pillar of strength to him. More successful than he was, she even referred him to several producers.

The author of the actor Mehmood's official biography, Hanif Zaveri, says, 'Amitabh and Anwar [Mehmood's brother] were close friends. Anwar told me that he had often taken Amitabh and Jaya on long drives. The two would sit in the front seat of the car along with him while Rekha would sit in the back seat and they would talk through the journey.' This is also recorded in Mehmood's official biography, *Mehmood: A Man of Many Moods*.

Even though Jaya and Rekha were competitors of sorts in the industry, Jaya was considered far more talented and was better respected. Asked to comment on Rekha in an interview, Jaya said that Rekha did not take herself seriously as a performer. It is believed that the interview did not go down well with Rekha.

In 1973 the Amitabh–Jaya starrer *Zanjeer* was released. After many flops, Amitabh made a blockbuster comeback in the industry. His portrayal of the Angry Young Man in *Zanjeer* set a new benchmark for success and established a new trend in the industry. After the triumph of this film, Amitabh and Jaya decided to get married.

On 3 June 1973, their wedding was solemnized. Rekha, however, was not invited, which left her feeling sour. In an interview, Rekha said, 'There was a time when I looked on Jaya as a sister… I used to think she was genuine, because she often spoke very seriously and gave me lots of loving advice. But now I realize that Jaya is a "general advisor" to every Tom, Dick and Harry. All she wants to do is to dominate people and that too, for only as long as it suits her.' Rekha did not stop there. She expressed resentment at not being called for the wedding: 'In spite of all her affectionate show of friendship and all that, she didn't even bother to invite me for her marriage – and my house was in the same building.'[2]

Jaya was now the bahu of the Bachchan household. She decided not to take on any new films but would finish the ones she had already signed.

~

The film-maker Dulal Guha had earlier made *Dushman* (1972) with Rajesh Khanna and *Dost* (1974) with Dharmendra and Shatrughan Sinha. Both films did well at the box office. He now wanted to attempt something unusual.

Guha decided to make *Do Anjaane* (1976), an adaptation of 'Ratrir Yatri', a story by Nihar Ranjan Gupta. It was about an ambitious girl who had starry dreams but was married off to a middle-class clerk. Her husband's wealthy friend then lures her and together they conspire to push him off a running train. The husband survives and later returns to avenge the hideous betrayal. Amitabh Bachchan was signed to play the lead and his friend's role was given to Prem Chopra. The heroine's character obviously had strong negative strains; by traditional Hindi film standards, she was a vamp. The role was offered to Sharmila Tagore and Mumtaz but both rejected it thinking it would ruin their image forever. Then Rekha was approached. After the narration of the script, she predictably wavered and told Guha, 'Dada, this is vampish.'

Guha insisted that the film centred on the female protagonist and that she would be well remembered for the role. His narration and insistence must have intrigued Rekha. Till then nobody had discussed the dimensions of a role seriously with her. So far she had been required mostly for cleavage-flashing song-and-dance routines and clichéd romantic scenes in her films. Despite having negative shades, this role seemed meatier than anything she had done. It was a risk though: she could be hated for the negative on-screen characterization or she could earn some respect as a multidimensional actress, something she had always craved. Rekha finally agreed.

At that time, she was mostly doing terrible B-grade films like *Wo Main Nahi* (1974), *Zorro* (1975) and *Dafaa 302* (1975). In big films like Feroz Khan's *Dharmatma*

(1975), she played second fiddle to Hema Malini. Even in Randhir Kapoor's *Dharam Karam* (1975), the focus was mainly on Raj Kapoor and Randhir Kapoor. *Do Anjaane* had the potential to earn her some credibility as an actress. So what if the role had negative shades?

Rekha's co-star in the film was Amitabh Bachchan, who was on a roll after *Zanjeer* and *Deewar* (1975). Plus he was Didibhai Jaya's husband. By then, the entire film industry was swearing by Amitabh's punctuality and professionalism, rare in the unorganized Hindi film industry. Gossip magazines thrived on stories about the tantrums of film stars and their incompetence, and Rekha's name constantly popped up in such stories; sincerity and punctuality were certainly not her strong suits. The unit of *Do Anjaane* was bracing for a clash.

But something altogether unexpected happened.

~

Amitabh always reached the sets on time. He rehearsed his lines and discussed the finer nuances of the character he was playing. His professionalism extended beyond shoot hours too: he would seldom stay back to party or drink. He chose to leave as soon as work was over and returned on time the next day.

Like everyone else, Rekha, too, was awestruck by Amitabh's persona. In her famous interview on *Rendezvous with Simi Garewal* in 2004, Rekha said, 'Standing in front of Mr Amitabh Bachchan is not easy.' She revealed that she was paranoid the moment she found out that Amitabh had been signed for *Do Anjaane*. The entire film industry was raving about his intense portrayal of the Angry Young Man in *Deewar*. Remembering that time, Rekha said that she was extremely nervous throughout the shoot of *Do Anjaane*. She light-heartedly recalled how she used to forget her lines out of nervousness and how one day, Amitabh told her in his baritone, '*Suniye...zara dialogue yaad kar lijiyega.*'

On *Rendezvous with Simi Garewal*, Rekha described Amitabh as 'something I'd never seen before. I've never met anyone like him. How can so many good qualities be bestowed on one person? I'm not a fool, I'm intelligent or so I'd like to believe. When I see a good thing, I can recognize it.'

Amitabh's dedication, sincerity and professionalism won Rekha over completely. He cast a spell on her, and the impact was clear for all to see.

Call it the Bachchan effect but Rekha now started doing something she had never done in her life: she arrived on the sets of *Do Anjaane* on time, at 6 a.m. sharp, much to everyone's surprise. But the change did not end there. She starting thinking deeply about the character she was essaying and discussed the finer points of the portrayal, much like Amitabh was wont to. Here was a man who was charismatic enough to be emulated.

The stage was set for a romance the industry would not stop talking about for decades.

~

Do Anjaane was based in Calcutta and a major month-long shoot was planned there. The lead stars of the film were staying at the famous Grand Hotel. Rekha was new to the city but Amitabh, having worked in Calcutta as an executive in a shipping firm called Bird & Co. before he joined films, knew Calcutta inside out. He had in fact spent eight years there from 1962 to 1969.

The heady romance of Calcutta rains was said to have done its bit in bringing the two stars closer. Amitabh used to narrate stories about the rustic charms of the city, and Rekha couldn't take her eyes off him. Film magazines went to town, quoting members of the *Do Anjaane* unit on post-shoot get-togethers. Rekha often visited the fabled Flurys tea room with Amitabh and Prem Chopra, walked along Park Street and dined out with them.

Many people associated with the unit of *Do Anjaane* still vividly recall the stark change they saw in Rekha. She was restrained in front of Amitabh; her youthful vivaciousness was replaced with a more measured gait.

~

Released on 1 January 1976, *Do Anjaane* wasn't a blockbuster, but the unusual storyline, powerful performances and Dulal Guha's crisp direction were commended in the industry and by critics.

The film remains underrated, partly because it has been overshadowed by Amitabh's iconic blockbusters of this period: *Sholay* (1975), *Deewar* (1975) and *Kabhi Kabhie* (1976). Films like *Adalat* (1976) and *Do Anjaane*, though critically acclaimed, didn't get much print space or audiences.

There was, however, something about *Do Anjaane* that didn't go unnoticed. For the first time in Rekha's career, she was taken seriously as an actress. *Film World* magazine reported, 'Rekha's done it. Smoothly, successfully. From a plump, pelvis-jerking, cleavage-flashing temptress, she has metamorphosed into a sleek, accomplished actress. Gone are most of the inane mannerisms, pouts, wiggles and giggles.' The report noted that her career prospects were significantly improved, as leading film-makers had started taking notice of her and were keen to sign her up. There were many other reviews on similar lines. Everyone was praising Rekha's performance and chemistry with Amitabh. This had never happened before.

Just this one film had led to new-found respect for Rekha. Respect. And Rekha gave the entire credit for this to Amitabh. He became the symbol of everything she had ever wanted in a man and Rekha was slowly falling in love with him. It didn't matter that he was taken. 'The fact that he was a married man doesn't make any kind of a difference. A rose is a rose is a rose. A human being is interesting, period. I want to have the honour of being associated with this person so what is stopping me? I'm not here to "break" his home, so to speak. I'm here to be one of the lesser mortals who can just have a whiff of him and feel happy,' Rekha said on the Simi Garewal show. The Superstar had completely swept Rekha off her feet.

But Amitabh never officially commented on this.

11

Makeover

'I became a vegetarian and stopped living dangerously.'
– Rekha

A metamorphosis was under way. Around 1976, Rekha, then in her early twenties, charted out a plan to change the way she looked and the way people saw her. In this industry, obsessed with the visual and nothing deeper, perception was everything. Rekha's sudden focus on self-improvement was a consequence of her new association with Amitabh Bachchan: quite likely she wanted to prove that she was his equal in every way, that she was worthy of him.

Gone was the free-spirited girl who took life as it came, seldom planned for the future and didn't care about her career trajectory. Rekha was no longer okay with struggling with Hindi, English and Urdu. She worked on, like never before, flattening the 'tyres', rolls of fat, around her midriff. She was focused not just on crafting a new face and look but also on carving out a brand new personality.

Rekha's transformation was a classic filmi story of a plain Jane turning into a glamorous diva, one of the most sensational real-life makeovers. From an average-looking, South Indian heroine to a style goddess hailed for her ageless beauty, Rekha accomplished a fairy-tale transformation in real life.

In the beginning, she went on fad diets. She would reportedly drink only milk for two months at a stretch, and took other such drastic measures that showed her resolve. A year later, a distinctly different Rekha emerged. The excess fat had been knocked off. Rekha followed a strict diet and a rigorous exercise routine. She led a disciplined life and even practised yoga – this was unheard of in the 1970s. In many ways, Rekha was a trendsetter, a trailblazer.

According to the veteran journalist and film-maker Khalid Mohamed, 'The audience was floored when there was a swift change in her screen personality, as well as her style of acting. This period marked the beginning of Rekha's physical transformation. She started paying attention to her make-up, dress sense, and worked to improve her acting technique and perfect her Hindi-language skills.'[1]

In the 1970s, make-up men used to follow antiquated and theatrical make-up techniques. The up-curved, exaggerated winged look at the corners of the eyes, coupled with copious amounts of mascara, made actresses look atrocious. Rekha realized that make-up is an extremely crucial part of show business and reportedly decided to go to London to learn the art of make-up at the Make-up School there. She also hired Meena Kumari's make-up man, Ram Dada, who worked with her till his death. 'Make-up is an art form. I saw that my features could be enhanced with the right make-up. I had atrocious long eyelashes in *Rampur Ka Lakshman* [1972]. I felt this was not me. But Ram Dada came to my rescue.'[2]

Despite losing weight, Rekha was always self-conscious and self-deprecating about her hips: 'I can't do anything about my hips. Even in my dreams where the rest of me becomes so beautiful, my hips remain big!'[3]

Rekha's makeover was much talked about. But she gave all the credit for it to the reigning superstar of that time. Through references, direct and indirect, she suggested that it was he who transformed her for the better. She repeatedly gushed about how Amitabh's entry into her life had triggered the dramatic change and made her what she had become.

'It is the strongest influence in my adult life, just like my mother was in my adolescence. From him I learnt punctuality, silence, discipline, dedication, concentration and professionalism. He influenced my behaviour and lifestyle. I became a vegetarian and stopped living dangerously. The enchanting thing is that with him, it's not just the change but even the process of changing that has been beautiful,'[4] she told Bhawana Somaaya.

Amitabh Bachchan never officially commented on this.

~

The mid 1970s, when stories of Rekha's alleged association with Amitabh started doing the rounds, was also a time when certain film magazines became particularly aggressive in their journalism. There were scoops every fortnight. *Stardust*, in particular, started probing deep into the personal lives of celebrities, leaving some of the big stars furious. Amitabh's proximity to the Gandhi family was well known and it was alleged that during the Emergency he used his influence to try to shut down or censor some film magazines, particularly *Stardust*.

Two years later, after the Emergency was lifted and Indira Gandhi had lost the elections, the editors of the five top-selling film magazines of the day, including *Stardust*, *Cine Blitz* and *Star & Style*, got together and decided that it was payback time: Amitabh Bachchan was 'banned' on their pages.[5] Recalling that phase, Amitabh wrote on his blog, '...the entire press went against me, because they were informed by "sources" that I...had brought on the idea of the Emergency and a ban on the press... Nothing could have been more ridiculous. But they did not relent and banned me; no interviews, no mention or pictures, or news of mine were ever printed in any form of the media during that time.'[6] Amitabh retaliated by banning the press from his life and from entering his sets.

This was the time that Amitabh's career skyrocketed and Rekha and Amitabh grew closer. There were stories about clandestine meetings between them. But given the 'ban' on him, how did the media report on these sensational developments? Amitabh was referred to variously as the 'Superstar' or 'Lambuji' or just plain 'he'.

This suited Rekha. She dropped ample hints about their growing fondness for each other and how Amitabh inspired her to do better. The shooting of Prakash Mehra's *Khoon Pasina* (1977), Hrishikesh Mukherjee's *Alaap* (1977) and *Immaan Dharam* (1977), films that Amitabh and Rekha were doing together, had begun, and Rekha made sure that stories of her and the Superstar were never out of circulation. She proclaimed, 'When I am in love, I'm in it completely – every minute of every hour I'm thinking about HIM. Twenty-four hours it's him, him, him in my thoughts. If he has promised to call at a particular time, and he doesn't, I bring the roof down. After all, if he couldn't make it, he shouldn't have promised at all, should he?'[7]

Prakash Mehra directed many of Amitabh's blockbuster films, and shared a close association with him. Apart from *Khoon Pasina*, Amitabh and Rekha worked in Mehra's most celebrated film, *Muqaddar Ka Sikandar* (1978). He was witness to their growing intimacy during the shooting of *Khoon Pasina*, which started right after *Do Anjaane*. In *Eurekha*, Prakash Mehra is quoted as saying: 'Amitabh is the man who made her, taught her how to talk, walk... how to present herself. Amitabh *ne* Rekha *ko ek* culture *deeya... usey ehsaas hua ke* (Amitabh cultured Rekha...she understood that) if she had to even walk with this man, if she had to work with this man, she would have to come up to his exacting standards. His English, his Hindi... how cultured he is...she learned whom to meet, whom not to meet, how to talk. It was under his influence that she grew as an actress and as a woman!'

Stories of the romance brewing between them were trickling in, and Rekha was hopelessly in love. She was completely unaware of how she was going down the same path that she had abhorred since childhood. Her mother's fate was knocking on her door.

She had forgotten that this was not her story alone. There was another important player: Rekha's Didibhai and Amitabh's wife, Jaya Bachchan.

~

Amitabh and Rekha were big names in the industry and it was obvious that an association between them would not stay under wraps for long. In 1977 Sultan Ahmad's dacoit flick, *Ganga Ki Saugandh* (1978), was being filmed near Jaipur. During an outdoor shoot, a huge crowd had gathered to catch a glimpse of the stars. But one man in the crowd kept passing lewd remarks at Rekha. Despite repeated warnings, his nastiness continued. Amitabh, known for his composure, is said to have lost his cool and beat up the man.

This started a gossip wildfire. Film magazines played up the incident and speculated about why 'the classy and sophisticated Amitabh' would get into a fist fight for Rekha. What was going on? What started as hushed murmurs about a romance between them got amplified and the rumour mills went into overdrive.

~

The year 1977 saw a whopping eleven releases of Rekha: *Saal Solvan Chadya, Ram Bharose, Kachcha Chor, Farishta Ya Qatil, Ek Hi Raasta, Dildaar, Chakkar Pe Chakkar* and *Aap Ki Khatir* and (with Amitabh Bachchan) *Immaan Dharam, Khoon Pasina* and *Alaap*. Most of these were rather forgettable. While Amitabh was at the zenith of his career, Hrishikesh Mukherjee's *Alaap* turned out to be a box-office disappointment. Amitabh played the rather contained character of a musician in conflict with his father, a stark contrast to his dramatic and loud characters in blockbusters like *Amar Akbar Anthony* and *Parvarish*, released the same year. *Alaap* was unarguably the biggest disaster of Amitabh's career till then.

In *Immaan Dharam*, perhaps for the first and only time in her career, Rekha played the part of a Tamil labourer. She was not paired opposite Amitabh, who for some reason had been cast opposite Helen. Rekha's co-star, so to speak, was Shashi Kapoor. Written by the hugely successful writer duo Salim–Javed, it too sank without a trace. In both *Immaan Dharam* and *Alaap*, Amitabh and Rekha were playing non-glamorous parts, far from their mainstream flamboyant roles. The scripts lacked melodrama as well as the customary filmi romance. This, clearly, did not go down well with the audience.

Finally, *Khoon Pasina*, directed by Rakesh Kumar, hit the screens and was a welcome respite for the lead pair. The film set a new watermark for a melodramatic romance, as is exemplified by the popular, if rather strange, line in which Amitabh tells Rekha, '*Tera husn meri taaqat, teri tezzi meri himmat... Is sangam se jo aulaad paida hogi, woh aulaad nahi faulaad hogi.*' (Your beauty is my strength. Your passion, my courage. Our union will give birth to men of steel, not wimpy children.) The rumours and stories of Rekha and Amitabh's real-life romance added to the audience's appreciation of their on-screen chemistry. There was raucous catcalling and wolf-whistling in cinema halls. Amitabh, called Tiger in the film, wrestled an actual tiger in what was called an 'item fight'; predictably, he won, and Rekha jubilantly broke into the super-hit romantic number, '*Tu mera ho gaya, main teri ho gayi*'. The couple married in a happy ending that the audience seemed thrilled with.

∼

Though Rekha tried her best to project an impeccably professional and polished image in front of the media, the list of producers harassed at her hand was still long. She was tailed by industry legend and lore of routine disappearances from shoots. Producers chided her for being callous towards work. While she did, on occasion, transform into a model of sincerity, these rare moments were reserved exclusively for films she did with Amitabh.

According to Randhir Kapoor, Rekha's co-star in several films and good friend, 'Rekha has been criticized for being untalented. But I know for sure that she's a bomb of talent. Her face, especially her eyes, are unbeatable. It's a pity she's not interested enough to improve her career. She concentrates more on her extra-curricular activities.'[8]

Simi Garewal echoed a similar sentiment in one of her interviews: 'As an actress she is ordinary. She could be really good if she worked at it.'[9]

The industry was unanimous in declaring Rekha irresponsible and disinterested in her career.

12

Ghar

'My love scenes were so convincing because I would just substitute Vinod Mehra for "him".' – Rekha

Despite her physical transformation, as an actress, Rekha remained ordinary and continued to sign a huge number of films; on average, she worked in ten films a year. Most of these were forgettable, at best. Try stretching your memory to see if any of these names rings a bell: *Aaj Ka Mahatma* (1976), *Ram Bharose* (1977), *Kachcha Chor* (1977), *Farishta Ya Qatil* (1977), *Ek Hi Raasta* (1977), *Rahu Ketu* (1978), *Ram Kasam* (1978) or *Parmatma* (1978). Rekha played the lead in all these films and several of them, interestingly, were also box-office successes. However, the intensity of performance that she was capable of, as seen in *Do Anjaane*, was missing.

If eleven films in 1977 is stupendous, 1978 saw an incredible fourteen releases of Rekha. Most of these films too have been wiped clean from public memory. However, one of these proved to be a watershed in Rekha's career. Any discussion on Rekha as an actress is incomplete without a mention of *Ghar*.

In *Ghar*, the newly-weds Aarti, played by Rekha, and Vikas, played by her former lover Vinod Mehra, were attacked while returning home from a night show. Vikas fainted, and on waking found out that Aarti had been gangraped. Aarti was, of course, severely traumatized, and the incident left a deep wound on the husband–wife relationship. Both grappled with the burden of their grief and drifted apart in the process. The film should be lauded for its realistic portrayal of the wounds rape can leave on a person's psyche, and how it can affect her associations with the outside world.

The almost-real on-screen chemistry between Rekha and Vinod was perhaps a vestige of their previous intimacy. Gulzar wrote some memorable lyrics for the film, including songs like '*Aapki Ankhon Mein Kuchh*' and '*Aaj Kal Paon Zameen Par Nahi*', which added to and strengthened the romance between the protagonists.

The delicate handling of emotional complexity and the way it has been woven into the story have the unmistakable imprimatur of Gulzar. The story behind this is rather interesting. The film's credits mention Manek Chatterjee as its director. But Manek met with an accident just after shooting began, and so the producer N.N. Sippy asked Gulzar to take over. Though the original script was written by Dinesh Thakur, Gulzar made significant interventions and changes to it. The nuances of the husband–wife relationship that was eventually portrayed in the film seem to draw a lot from the sensibilities of the writer-director Gulzar.

However, one also needs to acknowledge Rekha's superlative acting: she showed the restraint that the character demanded and gave a truly mature performance. Her eyes, vivid and alive when singing *'Aaj kal paon zameen par nahi padte mere'* became hauntingly empty with despair, dead almost, when she played the rape survivor. The possessed look she had when she attempted suicide and her forlorn expression when she was dreading the loss of love were in keeping with Aarti's character, which Rekha realistically and movingly depicted. Was this the same woman whose signature dance step was the pelvic gyration? Was this demure, sari-clad, shy woman the 'sex kitten' of the industry? In Gulzar's hands, Rekha rendered an unbelievable performance, and silenced her critics in the industry.

Misty-eyed with memories, Gulzar expresses honest appreciation for Rekha's talent: 'This is the quality of the artist: how do they put on the character? How does he or she clothe himself completely in the given character… *Woh us kirdaar ko libaas ki tarah pahen leti hai.*[1] (She is able to get into the character like a dress.)

While filming the rape scene in *Ghar*, Gulzar had instructed Rekha and the four stuntmen playing the rapists to improvise where they thought fit. It is said that Rekha performed this scene with such passion that Gulzar refused to dub it later. He felt that the expressions and emotions portrayed by Rekha could not be improved on, and the scene was used in the film with the original audio.

Ghar proved how Rekha could prosper as an actress in the hands of an able director. That was the first time she had worked with Gulzar. The first day of the shoot came on the heels of the release of *Aandhi* (1975), which was directed by Gulzar. Gulzar, who had a reputation for punctuality, reminisces about that day: 'It wasn't that we had met through films. She was a great favourite of Rakhee's [Gulzar's actress wife], was her pet, and hence we'd met many times at home also.' Given their frequent interactions, Rekha was well aware of Gulzar's nature.

On the first day of shooting, however, Rekha was really late. She came in after lunch, and though Gulzar continued with the shoot for the day, he prodded her after it had wound up. 'I affectionately call her Kaalo Babu. With a lot of love, I asked her the reason for her delay.' Rekha's response is a running joke between them: she had been away to watch *Aandhi* because she wanted to be prepared in case it cropped up in conversation. But Gulzar immediately caught her out by asking, 'You wanted to be prepared for conversations or desired to check how good is the director?' Gulzar laughs as he remembers this exchange.

Though Rekha's *Ghar* co-star Vinod Mehra was a

former lover of hers, rumours of her affair with Amitabh kept finding their way into print. While the romantic scenes in *Ghar* got much praise, Rekha explained her amazing chemistry with her co-star by alluding to Amitabh: 'My love scenes were so convincing because I would just substitute Vinod Mehra for "him".'[2]

'He' would become a recurring figure in Rekha's media interactions; she deliberately slipped in casual references to Amitabh at every opportunity and kept him in the audience's imagination.

Amitabh Bachchan never responded to Rekha's comments and always denied the alleged relationship about which so much was written for years.

13

Zohrabai

'It is not a question of what does Jaya have that I don't have. What does Jaya have that I have?' – Rekha

While *Ghar* was an exercise in performative brilliance, *Muqaddar Ka Sikandar* (1978) proved, if any proof were required at all, that glitz and glamour were as much a part of Rekha's star persona. Rekha was not even the lead heroine in the latter but her chemistry with Amitabh was electrifying. She played the courtesan Zohrabai in the film, while the female lead was played by Rakhee. Interestingly, that year Rekha did another cameo role in an Amitabh film, *Kasme Vaade* (1978), in which she again played a courtesan, and Rakhee was the female lead. Both these films, *Kasme Vaade* and *Muqaddar Ka Sikandar*, were huge hits, but the latter emerged as a record-breaking box-office success story.

In *Muqaddar Ka Sikandar*, Rekha wore an iconic

electric pink outfit as she sang '*Salaam-e-ishq meri jaan zara qubool kar lo*'. This was a break from the past and foretold things to come. There was a new intensity in her eyes as she raised her hand in a graceful salaam, in stark contrast to her trademark lurid gyrating. Her dance movements became more fluid, with a controlled *adaa* that exuded Lucknawi *tehzeeb* (culture). In *Kasme Vaade*, however, audiences again saw the old Rekha, ringlets framing her face, with a marked absence of adaa. Rekha's hair, make-up, jewellery, clothing and dance style in '*Salaam-e-ishq*', the mammoth hit song of 1978, were but a hint of things to come – they were highly refined and deployed to great effect in her ultimate portrayal of the courtesan in *Umrao Jaan* (1981).

In her small but memorable role as Zohrabai, Rekha brought depth to the character of a courtesan, the proverbial 'other woman'. She brought alive the human side of a tawaif, embellishing her with style, grace and a certain delicate charm. Her scenes with Amitabh are the most dramatic in the film, even though Zohrabai's character had nothing to do with the central plot. In Rekha's opening scene, the heartbroken Sikandar, played by Amitabh, finds solace in the arms of the courtesan Zohrabai. While Zohra's heart melts for Sikandar, she herself is the object of Dilawar's (Amjad Khan's) obsession. Dilawar is a gangster and also Sikandar's nemesis in the film. Rekha's cameo was confined to a few scenes and songs, but her chemistry with Amitabh outshone everything else.

Jerry Pinto says, 'Rekha, I think, arrived at her peak in *Muqaddar Ka Sikandar*. This is the biggest and most beautiful film that she ever did. [Director] Prakash Mehra, when he was making it, said people said I am a fool because…everybody dies in the end of this film and the people who are left behind are the most colourless of the characters [Vinod Khanna and Rakhee]. Rakhee at this point was way past her prime.'

Prakash Mehra said, 'Rekha had that spark. She has never got the right role. It was during the final narration of the story that we thought of this variation of the old Devdas type of song… I had observed Rekha and thought that she fitted the role perfectly. She became Zohrabai and till today, I call her Zohrabai.'[1]

~

Rekha never spoke much about her performance in *Muqaddar Ka Sikandar*. When she did, though, she referred to the role as one of the closest to her heart. In many ways, Zohrabai's fate was also her fate.

In one of her rare interviews on the film, she told the journalist Dinesh Raheja, 'The *MKS* [*Muqaddar Ka Sikandar*] phase was the blooming of my womanhood. And I think it was the beginning of the most beautiful phase of my life. It was a period of self-discovery.'[2]

This self-discovery, perhaps, alluded to Rekha's predilection for such roles. The depiction of a nautch girl or courtesan remained formulaic in Bollywood for many decades. This courtesan is usually possessed of a golden heart, and believes in selling her art, not her body or, by extension, her soul. She often ends up falling for the hero and, akin to Devdas's Chandramukhi, remains devoted to him without expectations of reciprocation. It is unlikely that one can name even a single mainstream film in which such a relationship culminates in marriage. The courtesan evokes sympathy in the viewers. They know that such a relationship could never be – either in real life or in films. This is why the end necessarily demands that either the courtesan dies or the hero does. Often, the hero is reunited with the 'chaste' heroine. The 'other woman' remains the outsider and ends up lonely.

Rekha performed the role of a courtesan or the 'other woman' on dozens of occasions. In many films, she appeared on screen just to perform a single song as a nautch girl. For years it was a running joke among filmmakers that if there was a role of a courtesan, Rekha would do it; she would love to be Zohrabai again.

Having witnessed the hardships her mother had to face, Rekha should have abhorred the role of the other woman. Yet, a major part of her career consisted of playing such roles. Many of Rekha's interviews and the events of her life leave one with a lingering feeling that she felt a strong connection with such characters and their loneliness. It was as if Zohrabai and Rekha were the same person.

~

Most people who had worked with Rekha at some bend of her career or the other willingly speak on almost all aspects of Rekha's life: her films, the ups and downs of her career, and even her supposed affairs, albeit in hushed tones. So were Rekha and Amitabh ever actually together? Many people in the industry believe that this story of love was never true.

By 1978, Rekha and Amitabh's alleged affair had found its way to the cover stories of most magazines. While many reckoned that the off-screen affair was a mere ruse, a convenient spin-off from their great on-screen chemistry exploited to garner as much publicity as possible for their films, others were only too happy to believe the spiced-up stories.

It was often reported that the supposed affair, not surprisingly, caused much turmoil in the Bachchan household. In this regard, the most revealing and astonishing interview is of Rekha herself. Today people don't ask Rekha such questions but in several old interviews, she talked rather openly about her love and the attendant risks. Not only did she speak about the intimacy between Amitabh and her but she didn't shy away from mentioning Jaya Bachchan by name, and her reaction to their purported affair.

In a sensational interview published in *Stardust* in 1978 – 'Rekha: Girl without a Conscience?' – Rekha claimed, 'Once I was looking at the whole [Bachchan] family through the projection room when they came to see the trial show of *Muqaddar Ka Sikandar*. Jaya was sitting in the front row and he and his parents were in the row behind her. They couldn't see her as clearly as I could. And during our love scenes, I could see tears pouring down her face.'[3] It is believed that Jaya put a ban on Amitabh working with Rekha after *Muqaddar Ka Sikandar*, and word got around fast that Amitabh had been given an ultimatum by his wife. Discussing this, Rekha said, 'A week later [after the trial show of *Muqaddar Ka Sikandar*], everybody in the industry was telling me that he has made it clear to his producers that he was not going to work with me. Everybody else informed me about it but he didn't say a word on the subject. When I tried to question him about it, he said, "I am not going to say a word. Don't ask me about it".'[4]

In the same interview, Rekha revealed another shocking detail: she claimed that Amitabh had gifted her two rings that she always wore. When Amitabh refused to work with her, she returned the rings and decided to part ways with him. In her own words, 'Naturally I was upset and we broke off after that. I was working in *Khoobsurat* at that time and I put my heart and soul into my role. You will notice that in the last half of the film I am not wearing my two rings. They have been given to me by him and I never remove them even when I am sleeping. But during those days when we had parted, I sent them back to him.'[5]

Rekha claimed that she was deeply hurt by Amitabh's decision not to work with her but it was Jaya who ended up becoming the target of her tirades. She melodramatically emphasized that her pain was somehow far greater than Jaya's. 'At an award function some time ago, I'd recited a few lines. Everyone imagined they were meant for him. But actually, it was for her,' said Rekha. Rekha recited the lines in the interview: 'I looked at you, you turned your face away. Why? You feel you are badly off, but can't you see my position is worse? There is deep hurt in your gaze, but can't you see that the wounds in my heart are deeper than your look?'6

Rekha, bold and direct, dropped all veils of secrecy. Whether she was telling the truth is difficult to determine, but her statements often caused an uproar at that time. She was seen as launching a head-on assault on the clean image of the Bachchans. Calling herself the 'other woman' for the first time, Rekha said, 'People say the wife is always one-up because she has the man. I say the "other woman" is ten-up because the man wants her in spite of having a wife. It is not a question of what does Jaya have that I don't have. What does Jaya have that I have?'7

Amitabh Bachchan never officially commented on this.

14

The Other Woman

'She gives the impression to men that she is easily available.'
– Nargis Dutt

Despite disturbances in her personal life, Rekha's career was touching new heights by the late 1970s. Though parallel cinema was throwing up some fine names like Shabana Azmi and Smita Patil, acclaim for them fell far short of popular cinema heroines like Hema Malini, Zeenat Aman and Rekha.

As always, Rekha was indiscriminately signing a large number of films but this time around the list included films by some exceptional directors: *Khoobsurat* (1980) by Hrishikesh Mukherjee, *Ram Balram* (1980) by Vijay Anand, *Kalyug* (1981) by Shyam Benegal, *Vijeta* (1982) by Govind Nihalani and the crown of her career, *Umrao Jaan* (1981) by Muzaffar Ali. As a lead actress, this was the golden phase of her career.

Rekha's success at the box office continued in 1979: besides *Ahimsa* and *Jaani Dushman*, she was paired with Dharmendra in the hugely successful *Kartavya*, directed by Mohan Sehgal, who had launched her in *Sawan Bhadon*. Earlier, Rekha and Dharmendra had done a bold romantic song in *Keemat* (1973); now again *Kartavya* had one of the most sizzling songs in the history of cinema, '*Doori Na Rahe Koi*'. Though Rekha had genuinely brilliant on-screen chemistry with Dharmendra, it was less talked about as more print space was devoted to her closeness to 'him'.

Amitabh Bachchan was, predictably, associated with the two Rekha films that created the most buzz in 1979: *Mr Natwarlal* and *Suhaag*. He was at the peak of his stardom, having only the previous year enjoyed the enormous success of *Don*.

Mr Natwarlal was a revenge drama spiked with whacky comedy. In the world of Hindi films, the coupling of an actor and actress is remembered till long after by the songs picturized on them. While in *Muqaddar Ka Sikandar*, the song '*Salaam-e-ishq*' became synonymous with Amitabh and Rekha's supposed affair, in *Mr Natwarlal*, it was '*Pardesiya Yeh Sach Hai Piya*' that was, for audiences, something of a public confession of their relationship.

Mr Natwarlal was directed by Rakesh Kumar, who had earlier worked with the pair in *Khoon Pasina*. In a 1999 interview,[1] he shared that the entire unit was baffled by Rekha's commitment to her work while shooting with

Amitabh. A few scenes of the film needed to be shot in Kashmir at sunrise. While this was no big deal for the punctual Amitabh, everyone was certain that Rekha wouldn't make it on time. Rakesh Kumar said that in order to reach the set on time, Rekha would wake up at 2 a.m. for make-up, and leave for the location by 4 a.m.

Film-makers of that time likely tried to exploit Rekha and Amitabh's alleged affair by including scenes that alluded to it. Take, for instance, a scene from *Mr Natwarlal* in which Rekha says to Amitabh, *'Mai teri daasi hoon.'* (I am your slave.) And he says, *'Mujhe koi daasi waasi nahi chahiye.'* (I don't want a slave.) According to Jerry Pinto, this scene was a shockingly real tableau of their actual lives: 'a *gaon ki gori* [an unrefined though beautiful woman] who's in the process of being transformed into a middle-class woman is offering her love and is being rejected'.

Her second hit of the year with Amitabh was *Suhaag*, a bundle of the director Manmohan Desai's usual tropes: the nautch girl, serendipity, separation and some racy songs like *'Athra Baras Ki Tu Hone Ko Aayi'* and *'Rab Ne Bana Di Jodi'*.

~

In a display of typically sexist hypocrisy, the film industry singled out Rekha and maligned her, not her partners, for her supposed relationships. After reports of affairs with Jeetendra, Dharmendra, Sunil Dutt and now Amitabh

Bachchan, among others, Rekha was being projected as a woman who posed a 'threat' to all married men. Derogatory labels like 'man-eater', 'nymphomaniac' and 'sex kitten' were used casually and callously to refer to her.

At the peak of her career, Rekha was at the receiving end of scathing attacks by other leading actresses. The acclaimed actress of her era Nargis Dutt said about Rekha in 1976: 'She gives the impression to men that she is easily available. Rekha is looked on as a "witch" by some. Sometimes I think I understand her. I've worked with a lot of children with a lot of psychological problems in my time. She's lost. She needs a strong man.'[2]

Dimple Kapadia is reported to have told Rekha to steer clear of Rajesh Khanna, saying 'stay away from my husband'.

Commenting on Rekha, Zeenat Aman told a film magazine, 'We should have got along better, because we have quite a few things in common, including the fact that we've both grown up without a father on the scene. But in her case she seems to be terribly insecure. She seems very frivolous and empty. About her looks; neck-upwards and with make-up on, she's quite stunning. Apart from that, neck-downwards, she really needs to work on herself.'[3]

The writer Khushwant Singh, however, known for his blunt wit, effortlessly attacked the double standards of the film industry: 'Rekha is probably the victim of the usual masculine habit of describing any woman who is stylish and uninhibited as a "nymphomaniac". Probably, it's also a kind of wishful thinking of the male. I admire people like Rekha and Protima Bedi. Only I wish they didn't indulge in it deliberately for publicity. Otherwise, the more scandalous Rekha's statements are, the more I like her.'[4]

And scandal she did create with her next move.

~

22 January 1980. The occasion was Rishi Kapoor and Neetu Singh's wedding. Neetu was a close friend of Rekha's. The whole of R.K. Studio was grandly bedecked to celebrate Raj Kapoor's son's wedding. The biggest names of the industry were in attendance, including Amitabh Bachchan, his wife, Jaya, and his parents. The party was in full flow. Amitabh was talking to Manmohan Desai in a corner and Jaya was sitting with her mother-in-law, Teji Bachchan, when Rekha made a sensational entry. All eyes turned at once towards her. Dressed in a magnificent white sari, Rekha had a bright red bindi on her forehead. But what caught everyone's eye was the generous dabbing of sindoor in her hair. The cameras instantly pivoted away from Rishi Kapoor and Neetu Singh, and frenetically photographed Rekha's curious new look. The dull drone of everyone murmuring and whispering filled the evening air; everyone wanted to know: had Rekha married?

Cine Blitz summed up the mood of the evening in its report: 'Don't miss the *sindoor* in her hair, which only married ladies wear. It's not something even people in films wear as a fashion. What is she trying to prove – that she's hooked?' According to the report, after congratulating Rishi and Neetu, Rekha went and stood bang in the middle of R.K. Studio's garden. When had she ever shied away from attention, or controversy? But her eyes kept darting towards Amitabh every other second. That evening, Amitabh had injured his hand and was wearing a bandage on it. Gathering courage, Rekha took hold of her close friend Snehlata Pandey, the doctor who is credited for introducing Rekha to aerobics and better diets, and went over to where Amitabh was standing. All eyes, quite naturally, followed her. They were seen chatting formally for a few minutes. According to a report in *Stardust*, 'Jaya tried to keep a stoic front for a long time, but eventually she had to bend her head and let the tears roll down.'[5]

A few moments later, Rekha exited the party, leaving behind a trail of unanswered questions that kept ringing in people's minds till weeks later. Pictures from that evening occupied much space in film magazines.

In a somewhat anticlimactic interview, Rekha later cleared the air: that evening, she had come to the reception straight from a shoot. The sindoor and mangalsutra she was wearing were part of her get-up for a film, which she had forgotten to remove.

But according to a report published in *Movie* in June 1982, at a National Awards function, Rekha, who was being honoured with the award for best actress for *Umrao Jaan* (1981), was asked by then president of India

Gold Spot advertisement (1969). Before any of Rekha's Bollywood films were out, she modelled for ads to earn extra money. This one was shot by Shyam Benegal.

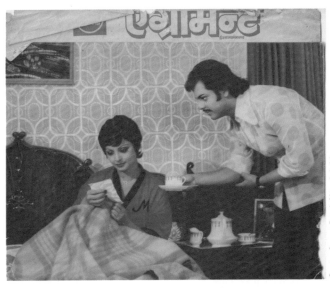

Previous spread, left top: Poster of *Agreement* (1980). Rekha was infamous for indiscriminately signing forgettable B-grade films such as this one, because she was often the only working member of her large family.

Left bottom: Poster of *Sawan Bhadon* (1970). Rekha's co-star Navin Nischol poked fun at her for her weight and skin tone. She was literally painted white for the film.

Right top: Poster of *Namak Haraam* (1973). This was Rekha's first film with Amitabh Bachchan, though they had no scenes together.

Right bottom: Poster of *Do Anjaane* (1976). This was Rekha and Amitabh's first major film together. During a month-long shoot in Calcutta, they were seen together at Flurys tea room, walking on Park Street and at dinners.

Above: Poster of *Ganga Ki Saugandh* (1978). Amitabh, Rekha's co-star in the film, reportedly beat up a bystander at an outdoor shoot near Jaipur for making lewd remarks at Rekha.

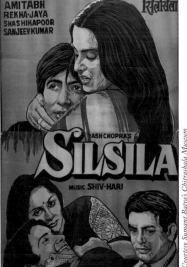

Courtesy Sumant Batra's Chitrashala Museum

Source: Super magazine (December 1980)

Anticlockwise from top right: Poster of *Mr Natwarlal* (1979). The film's unit was apparently baffled by the usually lax Rekha's sincerity and punctuality while shooting with Amitabh.

Poster of *Ram Balram* (1980). Starring both Rekha and Amitabh, the film didn't do well and marked a low point in Amitabh's career. The press had begun to write him off.

Amitabh and Rekha at a shoot.

Poster of *Silsila* (1981). Through the shooting of this film starring Amitabh, Rekha and Jaya Bachchan, the director Yash Chopra feared a clash between Jaya and Rekha. At one point, shot incomplete, Rekha reportedly walked off the sets.

Source: Super magazine

A full-page spread of Rekha in *Super* magazine (December 1980). The accompanying text mentioned her 'one very special man', as well as her unprofessionalism on film sets.

Top: Rekha and Naseeruddin Shah on the sets of *Umrao Jaan* (1981), the crowning glory of her career. Rekha won the National Award for best actress for the film.

Bottom: Rekha on the sets of *Umrao Jaan*. Though he was not working in the film, Amitabh Bachchan spent much time on its sets in Delhi, according to the director Muzaffar Ali.

Poster of *Umrao Jaan*. Rekha was criticized for the premiere of the film being held at a time when Amitabh Bachchan was critically injured and in hospital.

Poster of *Utsav* (1984). Publicized as a semi-erotic film, *Utsav* was seen as Rekha's desperate attempt to counter a new brigade of younger actresses. It flopped.

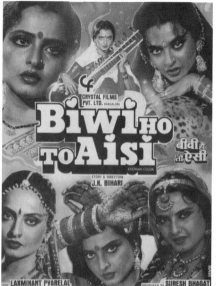

Top: Poster of *Biwi Ho To Aisi* (1988). The film marked Rekha's comeback after a rough patch in the mid 1980s. It was also Salman Khan's debut film.

Bottom: Poster of *Khoon Bhari Maang* (1988). This cult favourite is known for its 1980s style and fashion. Rekha was thrown into a lake of crocodiles by Kabir Bedi in the film; she survived, had a plastic surgery makeover, and took her revenge.

Courtesy Mala Kumar

Courtesy Mala Kumar

Rekha and Mukesh Agarwal at their friend Neeraj Kumar's house in Delhi in 1990. Mukesh was a businessman who was known to mount an enormous stallion to receive guests at his farmhouse in Delhi. To everybody's shock, Rekha married Mukesh on 4 March 1990 in Bombay.

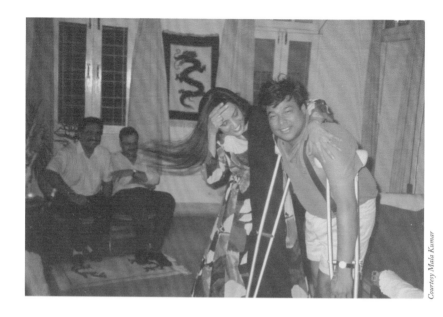

Top: Akash Bajaj and Mukesh Agarwal in the late 1980s. Before Mukesh married Rekha, he was reportedly involved with his psychotherapist Akash Bajaj, who had been treating him for depression. Mukesh ultimately committed suicide on 2 October 1990, after his marriage with Rekha broke down.

Bottom: Rekha with her secretary Farzana and Saawan Kumar at an award function in 2008. Mukesh's family blamed Farzana for the breakdown of his marriage to Rekha and for his suicide. They alleged that Farzana and Rekha were romantically involved.

Poster of *Sheshnaag* (1990). After Mukesh's suicide, people vandalized *Sheshnaag* posters and blackened Rekha's face on them.

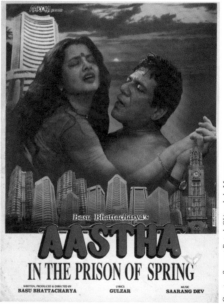

Top: Poster of *Madam X* (1994). The film, shot a couple odd years after Mukesh's death, is remembered for its outrageous costumes and styling. Rekha's career as a heroine was decisively over by that time.

Bottom: Poster of *Aastha* (1997). Rekha played a bored housewife who became a prostitute in this film known for its explicit love scenes.

Rekha and Farzana at Esha Deol's wedding reception in Bombay in 2012. Farzana can be seen wearing her trademark androgynous suit. Her appearance has been compared to that of Amitabh Bachchan's.

Rekha and Jaya Bachchan applauding Amitabh at the Star Screen Awards in Mumbai in 2016. Rekha made her way over to Jaya when Amitabh went on stage to collect the best actor award for *Piku* (2015).

Neelam Sanjiva Reddy, 'Why do you have *sindoor* in your *maang*?' The audience waited with bated breath. Rekha promptly replied into the mike, 'In the city I come from, it's fashionable to wear *sindoor*.'

~

Around the same time, Dharmendra got married to his long-time girlfriend Hema Malini in a secret ceremony. Dharmendra was already married and had four children from his first wife, Prakash Kaur. He never divorced Prakash, but Hema and he had converted to Islam in order to marry each other. News of their clandestine marriage was leaked and the film journalist A.T. Jayanthi broke the story in a smashing cover for *Star & Style*. There were stories in *Stardust* suggesting that when Rekha heard about Hema and Dharmendra's clandestine wedding, she became hopeful for herself: *'Ab mera bhi rasta niklega'* (now, there will be a way out for me too) was what she reportedly told Snehlata Pandey.

But in an interview much later, Jaya Bachchan, in fact, completely refuted her husband's involvement in any affair: 'Let the whole world say what they want. He [Amitabh Bachchan] has made a commitment to me and he has to have the courage (to say he's in love with somebody else!), and if he is doing something behind my back, it's his problem. Not my problem. He has to live with it. And with his conscience!'[6]

Without taking Rekha's name, Amitabh responded to the reported tensions in his marriage: 'A divorce will never happen in our case. I don't believe in divorce because my basic instincts are Indian. I made an absolutely first class choice when I took Jaya as my wife.'[7] This is the closest that Amitabh ever came to even admitting that all was not well in the Bachchan household.

But Rekha kept fuelling the media fire. In an interview to *Stardust*, she made a strange claim: that Jaya had invited her over to the Bachchan home one day. 'Jaya did not mind the relationship as long as she thought her husband was only having a fling. It's when she realized that he was really emotionally involved, that is when it began hurting her. She called me for dinner one evening and though we spoke about everything but him, before I left that day, she made sure to tell me, "I will never leave Amit whatever happens".'[8]

Scandalous disclosures were part and parcel of being Rekha. But this anecdote about an encounter between the wife and the mistress was truly sensational; and Jaya never refuted it. Whether this really happened is difficult to ascertain but a similar episode featuring the very same lead players was about to unfold on screen. The stars were about to align to bring Jaya, Amitabh and Rekha together on film, in spite of the promise that Jaya had extracted from Amitabh never to act with Rekha again.

A new *silsila* was soon going to unfold, bringing to life the hushed-up love triangle.

15

Queen

'When the audiences flocked to see it [Khoobsurat] *and rave over Rekha's performance do they remember Rekha's attachments to Vinod Mehra or Amitabh?'* – Bunny Reuben

Rekha's peak years as an actress were, undoubtedly, 1980 and 1981. During this time, she had many successful films and also experimented with parallel cinema, a genre she hadn't touched till then in her career.

After Hema Malini, then regarded as the Number One heroine in Indian cinema, married Dharmendra, she accepted fewer and fewer films, leaving the field wide open for Rekha. Though Zeenat Aman and Parveen Babi were among the other successful names in the industry, Rekha outpaced them by delivering good performances, starting with Hrishikesh Mukherjee's *Khoobsurat* (1980). Though the film did not boast of big stars, Rekha's comic timing and chirpy screen presence made it special.

Khoobsurat was followed by a hat-trick of melodramatic hits with Jeetendra and the director T. Rama Rao, *Judaai* (1980), *Maang Bharo Sajna* (1980) and *Ek Hi Bhool* (1981). Rekha also gave notable performances in Saawan Kumar's *Saajan Ki Saheli* (1981) and Ramesh Talwar's *Baseraa* (1981). This string of successes helped Rekha clinch the throne of the queen of Bollywood. She had found a new identity as an actor to be reckoned with. After over a decade in films, she had finally scaled the peak of the industry.

~

Rekha held Hrishikesh Mukherjee in high regard and shared a close bond with him. He endearingly called her Chinnapunnu, which means youngest daughter in Tamil. He had earlier directed Rekha in *Namak Haraam* (1973) and *Alaap* (1977). But Rekha did not have a major role in *Namak Haraam*, and though *Alaap* was a serious film, and a departure from Rekha's usual projects, it flopped miserably. Rekha had been eager to do another film with Hrishikesh Mukherjee and when Hrishida told her that he was planning a comedy that would be centred on the female lead, Rekha accepted the project.

In *Khoobsurat* Hrishikesh Mukherjee sculpted Rekha into the character of a free-spirited girl, Manju, who did not like to be tied down by boundaries. The plot got interesting when the effervescent Manju went to her elder sister Anju's discipline-obsessed *sasural* (in-laws' house). That household was run by a condescending matriarch, Anju's mother-in-law, a no-nonsense woman who liked to run a tight ship with clockwork precision. In that realm of order, Manju infused chaos, as she chanted *'Saare niyam tod do'* (break all the rules) and encouraged everyone to follow their heart towards *'nirmal anand'* (blissful happiness).

Khoobsurat was the first film of its kind for Rekha. While it did have some veteran actors, Rekha was the only 'star' in the cast. For the first time, a film was centred entirely on her. She was the focus of all the film posters.

Hrishikesh Mukherjee had told Rekha that the film would be made on a rather tight budget and there wouldn't be dozens of expensive costumes for her. In fact, Mukherjee had told Rekha, 'You give me twenty-five outfits of yours. You know the story; you know what will look good on you. I want you to be your real self, wear what you love to wear and leave the clothes with me till the film is released.' Rekha happily obliged.

Her look – simple dresses and hair in two plaits – was a huge success and set a trend of sorts that young girls all over the country emulated. Rekha apparently identified with the spirited nature of her character and called Manju 'quite a bit [like] me'.

The film journalist Bunny Reuben observed that Rekha was the only 'star' name in an otherwise 'small' movie and that it had no 'opening draw'. Yet *Khoobsurat* did better and better after its release thanks to word-of-mouth publicity. 'Because the film was terrific, because Rekha as the central character was terrific. When the audiences flocked to see it and rave over Rekha's performance do they remember Rekha's attachments to Vinod Mehra or Amitabh? Do they remember her *bindass* style of life and love? Do they hold it against her as an actress?'[1] asked Reuben. The answer was no. Gulzar recalls, 'Changing the body language denotes the success of an artist. Watch *Ghar*, on the one hand, and *Khoobsurat*, on the other; both are completely different. In *Khoobsurat*, you can glimpse boyishness in her [Rekha]. Watch *Khoobsurat* intensely, and you'll notice she's playing a boy. Isn't it?'[2]

Khoobsurat was a huge professional triumph for Rekha. It won her her first Filmfare Award for best actress (1981). The film also bagged the Filmfare Award for best film.

~

The 1981 Saawan Kumar film, *Saajan Ki Saheli*, had Nutan and Rajendra Kumar in lead roles. Both of them were on a downward trajectory in their careers. Therefore, Rekha's presence in the film helped in its publicity, and it too ended up doing fairly well. Vinod Mehra was Rekha's co-star in the film but despite a bitter past Rekha maintained cordial relations with him. According to Saawan, who has known Rekha since when she was close to Vinod Mehra, she was a woman who honoured and sustained relationships. Years later, she met Vinod again on the sets of Saawan's *Souten Ki Beti* (1989), along with his wife Kiran. She greeted them both warmly. For Rekha, the relationship might have ended, the connection had not.

Saawan is very fond of Rekha, whom he affectionately calls Baba. According to him, when he was directing *Hawas* (1974), he played Rekha a song that had been recorded for the film. Saawan wanted to film the song on Faryal, an actress who typically played the vamp in films. After listening to the song, Rekha said she wanted to perform on it. But Saawan said, 'Baba, it would be my good fortune that you do this song. However, the budget for the film is very less. We'll work together some other time.' 'Don't worry about the money,' Rekha replied. Not only did she perform on the song, '*Aao Yaaron Gaao*', for free, she also used her own costume, wig and jewellery. Saawan never forgot this unusually kind gesture. 'She is [a] good-hearted woman. I don't know if I should say this or not, but I am saying it: people have always played with her heart. Probably because of it she has now become smarter and stricter,' Saawan said. He added, 'She was very innocent and carefree earlier, but has changed a lot due to her experiences through life.'[3]

16

'Silsila'

'I was always on tenterhooks and scared [during the making of Silsila*] because it was real life coming into reel life. Jaya is his wife and Rekha is his girlfriend; the same story is going on. Anything could have happened because they are working together.'* – Yash Chopra

Rekha, still in her twenties, was at her peak in the early 1980s. She had arrived as a respected actress and a box-office sensation who had A-list producers queuing up to sign her. This Rekha bore no resemblance to the young Bhanurekha of ten years ago. Rekha was now constantly in the news for her beautiful cover shots, her fitness routine and her elusive lover. While Amitabh Bachchan had excommunicated the media from his life, it was Rekha who dedicatedly kept him alive in gossip columns and industry news. When Amitabh's career showed signs of instability, he again turned to Rekha.

In 1980, two of Amitabh's multi-star films, *Ram Balram* (1980) and *Do Aur Do Paanch* (1980), turned out to be box-office debacles. He then pinned his hopes on *Dostana* (1980), which, to his despair, didn't bring the relief he was looking for. The media had begun prophesying the doom of the star, who they believed had lost that special touch that made his films invincible at the box office.

In the same boat as Amitabh, the celebrated director-producer Yash Chopra had also been experiencing a rough patch. His last ambitious multi-starrer, *Kaala Patthar* (1979) featuring Amitabh Bachchan, performed miserably at the box office. He was reportedly shattered when the audience rejected this film, especially because it was close to his heart. He knew that his next film would have to be extraordinary. This gave birth to the idea of *Silsila*.

Amitabh immediately agreed to do the film, which was based on a love triangle. But Yash Chopra had bigger plans for *Silsila*. He suggested that Rekha be cast to play the role of the girlfriend. Despite his promise to Jaya that he would never work with Rekha again, Amitabh agreed. An announcement appeared in trade papers and in no time the film became the talk of the town. People were shocked – but delighted.

After her marriage to Amitabh, Jaya had busied herself with her household. She had two lovely children whom she was devoted to. This successful and extremely respected actress of her time seemed to have no intention of coming back to films. But according to *Stardust*, 'Jaya had given her husband the ultimatum, the biggest weapon in her armoury, that if he were to do a single film more with Rekha, she would rejoin films herself.'[1] With *Silsila* on the cards, Jaya prepared to act on her ultimatum. She did not simply sit pretty as her husband's name began hitting the tabloids alongside Rekha's.[2] Rather, she began the groundwork for her return and is known to have sent out feelers to close friends and co-stars.

But, then, along came Nellie.

~

Amitabh was shooting for his film *Laawaris* (1981) in Natraj Studio. Amitabh's alleged friendship with a new Iranian actress, Nellie, became the subject of gossip on the film sets and was written about in many magazines. This is said to have become the cause of serious conflict between Rekha and Amitabh. According to the *Laawaris* director Prakash Mehra, 'It was at Natraj Studio, on my sets. There was a heated exchange of words between her [Rekha] and Amitabh. She cried some more. I called her and told her to take it easy. All this drama was over Nellie.'

Stardust went to the extent of writing that there was a 'slapping and beating' incident.[3]

The drama around Nellie proved near fatal for *Silsila*:

an agitated and slighted Rekha decided to walk out of the film and immediately returned the signing amount.

Yash Chopra now had a hero and an ambitious film, but nothing else.

~

Reluctantly, Yash Chopra again began the hunt for female leads. At first, Padmini Kolhapure was signed to play the character of the 'other woman' and Poonam Dhillon's name was being mulled over for the role of the wife. But this casting did not please Yash; it wasn't what he had imagined for the film. Thereafter, he signed Parveen Babi as Rekha's replacement and Smita Patil as the betrayed wife. The cast in place, the first shoot of the film was scheduled in Kashmir.

Despite the film being on course, Yash Chopra was ill at ease. This was not the blockbuster cast he had hoped for. There was no selling point, nothing that would make the audience sit up and take notice. Yash wanted to grab headlines, but the Amitabh Bachchan–Parveen Babi–Smita Patil ensemble just did not have the edge that would send gossip columns into a tizzy. What Yash truly wanted seemed an impossible ask. In a memorable TV interview of Yash Chopra, his last before he died, with Shah Rukh Khan, the latter remarked: 'It was one of the most interesting, one of the biggest, one of the most challenging casts in a film ever done in the history of Indian cinema.'

How did it come about?

~

While Amitabh was shooting for Tinnu Anand's *Kaalia* (1981) in Srinagar, Yash Chopra flew down to meet him. On the night of 21 October 1980, they met over dinner. Yash shared in his interview with Shah Rukh Khan, 'After everyone [had] gone out of the room, he [Amitabh Bachchan] comes to me [and asks], "Are you sure with the casting of the film? Are you happy?" I said I am not happy. Bachchan asked, "You tell me honestly *ki aapko kya lagta hai iski* ideal casting *kya hai*."' (Tell me honestly what you feel the ideal casting for this film is.)

This gave Yash the opening he was hoping for. Yash said he wanted Rekha for the role of the other woman and Jaya to play the wife. Apparently, Yash threw in some bait and promised Amitabh a memorable film if he got the leading ladies of his life to play the leading ladies in this story. This was the first time in Indian cinema that the central plot revolved around an extramarital relationship. It deserved a cast that was capable of creating ripples at the box office.

Amitabh mulled over the suggestion for five minutes. He then suggested they go back to Bombay. Instead of asking her himself, Amitabh said Yash should persuade his wife to come on board. The next day, 22 October, both left for Bombay; there was a tense silence throughout the flight. Things were not going to be easy.

Reminiscing about the chaos created by the casting hassles, the writer of the film, Sagar Sarhadi, said, 'Jaya had extracted the promise from Amitabh that he would never work with Rekha. This was confirmed. Industry knew it. People knew it. This was a strange *dharam sankat* [moral dilemma].'[4]

Jaya and Rekha both had to be brought on board, despite the former being dead set against the idea of her husband working with the latter. How, then, was Jaya persuaded to work in the same film with the other two? How did *Silsila* become Jaya's much-awaited comeback? And how was Rekha lured back into the film?

~

Jaya, expectedly, was extremely reluctant to star in the film. In fact, it took much coaxing and cajoling to get her to even listen to the story. All through the narration, Jaya sat unmoved, looking neither interested nor impressed. Till the climax. It is said that it was the last scene that did the trick and moved Jaya to accept the role.[5] The climax of *Silsila* was a banal nuptial reunion: an unconscious Jaya lies on a hospital bed, doctors and nurses frantically trying to revive her. Just then, Amitabh enters and asks them to leave the room, saying, 'I know what is the matter, the remedy, leave us.' When alone, he places his palm lovingly on her forehead and gently takes her hand in his. He murmurs affectionately, 'Shobha, I have come back to you, forever.' At this, Jaya slowly opens her eyes and weakly says, 'I knew you would come back to me.' It is a moment that signified the victory of *vishwaas* (faith) over *pyaar* (love).

One is tempted to speculate about the resonance these words and sentiments would have had for Jaya. Perhaps this role, through which Jaya could both make a strong moral statement and help Amitabh's flailing career, seemed a good enough reason to re-enter films. According to Jerry Pinto, 'At some level they are all brutally callous about what will work at the box office. They don't really care. I mean think of *Silsila*. When he [Amitabh Bachchan] was doing *Silsila* the children were old enough to know what was going on and he went and signed the film.'

Super magazine did a cover story titled 'Jaya Is Back!' It said, 'Yash, whose dilemma of casting was fast exceeding human endurances, must've slept well for the first night in months on October 23rd, the happy day when Jaya agreed to his desperate, last measure request. Yash confesses, "I had a tough time getting her into the film."'

According to Sagar Sarhadi, 'It was decided...to explain everything to Jaya, because otherwise, this film couldn't be made. The compromise was Jayaji was asked to do Smita Patil's role and her permission was sought before signing Rekha.'

Rekha herself did not hesitate to block a few months of her shooting schedule for *Silsila*, perhaps because Nellie was reportedly not on the scene any longer.

~

An unspoken tension and competition had forever existed between Jaya and Rekha. Jaya had always been one up as far as acting was concerned. With Rekha, the reigning actress in the industry, now being pitched against her, a public battle was expected to follow.

In characteristic scandalous fashion, Rekha declared in an interview, 'I have learnt to use all the insults and barbs thrown at me to my advantage... Until you're provoked you don't realize your real value. The biggest contribution of this person in my life, for which I will remain eternally indebted to her, is that she taught me that no matter what happens, you should never give up your career. She is a living example of how you suffer if you do... Watching her, I've learnt not to be a hypocrite. That is why I am not a so-called martyr.'[6] It was clear to everyone who Rekha was referring to.

Yash Chopra was a relieved man but Rekha's sudden commitment of dates for *Silsila* left other producers upset. She had earlier committed the same dates for *Daasi* (1981), with Sanjeev Kumar, and Aamir Khan's father Tahir Hussain's *Locket* (1986). She gave preference to *Silsila* over both. While she did return from *Silsila* to complete the dubbing for *Daasi*, *Locket* took five years to complete and Hussain suffered huge losses and great agony at Rekha's hands. He never forgave her.

~

Thus the greatest Bollywood 'casting coup' was achieved. Amitabh, Jaya and Rekha were to essay the lead roles for *Silsila*. It caused quite a stir in the industry – no surprises there. Many provocatively remarked that the wife and the mistress had united to save Amitabh's career. While some were praising Yash Chopra for making the impossible happen, others used the opportunity to target Amitabh. His rival and former superstar Rajesh Khanna referred to the decision as 'a height of desperation'. He proudly narrated an episode that took place when his own career was 'in the gutters'. At a party thrown by Shomu Mukherjee, the producer Gulshan Rai had taken Dimple Kapadia aside and told her, 'Only you can save your husband's career by working in a film with him.' Dimple replied, 'If I have to even *suggest* such a thing to my husband, he will commit suicide.'

Regardless of the controversy, the cast and team of *Silsila* left for Kashmir.

17

Love Triangle

'As artists, we were acting out a story written for us; the rest existed in the imagination of the press and those who believe whatever's written in the magazines.' – Jaya Bachchan[1]

The shooting of *Silsila* began in Kashmir. It was an extremely private affair. No media was invited; no friends were permitted. Yash Chopra had to be very careful. He is said to have had to keep the two women as far away from each other as possible to avoid any clashes. Every scene had to be manoeuvred with precision. Later he said, 'I was always on tenterhooks and scared because it was real life coming into reel life. Jaya is his wife and Rekha is his girlfriend; the same story is going on. Anything could have happened because they are working together.'[2] Coming from someone of Yash Chopra's stature, this statement can't be taken lightly. He said, clearly and directly, that the Rekha–Amitabh relationship existed not only in gossip columns but in reality, too. Yash talked about it again in his famous interview with Shah Rukh Khan.

He told Shah Rukh, 'Before I started [shooting] the film, *maine dono ko alag alag [bola] – ikattha milna toh mushkil hi tha* for obvious reasons – *ki yaar dekho tum mere dost ho, tum meri* picture *mein kaam kar rahe ho dosti mein. Yaar mere* set *pe koi gadbadi mat karna yaar. Dono ne mujhe* surety *dilai bilkul* problem *nahi hogi.* [Before I started shooting the film, I told them both separately – it was difficult to meet them together for obvious reasons – that you are my friend, you are acting in my film out of friendship. Please don't do anything controversial on my set. Each assured me that there would be no problems.] And they didn't give me trouble.'

~

According to reports, Rekha, as a rule, tried to avoid Jaya by timing her exits with Jaya's entries. However, at times, all three, Amitabh, Jaya and Rekha, were forced to come together to shoot. When this happened, they would sit separately, like strangers, without communicating and wore blank expressions. One wouldn't believe this upon watching the film; each actor's performance shines brilliantly. This speaks volumes about the talent of the cast.

The embargo on the press could not, however, keep gossip from spilling over into magazine pages. A report in *Cine Blitz*, 'Inside the Making of *Silsila*', revealed some details: for a certain sequence, Jaya was required to cry, so she asked for some glycerine. Surprised that an actress of Jaya's calibre should need glycerine, a senior unit member reportedly asked her, Jayaji, *kya aap ko bhi* glycerine *ki zaroorat hai?*' (Jayaji, do you really need glycerine?) To this she retorted, '*Itna ro chuki hoon ki ab aur rone ke liye aansoon hi nahi bache hain.*' (I've cried so much already that I have no tears left.)

~

Among the many intense scenes, there is one in which Rekha and Jaya come face-to-face, and a dramatic verbal exchange takes place between them. This scene was probably scripted to cash in on the well-known tension between the actresses. The tussle between matrimony and extramarital love, and between faith and passion, form the core of this scene. Jaya, the quintessential wife wearing red, asked Rekha, in pristine white, to leave her husband, for she knew that her faith in their marriage would triumph over all else. At this, Rekha quipped, '*Aap apne vishwaas ke saath rahiye, mujhe mere pyaar ke saath rehne dijiye.*' (You hold on to your faith, let me hold on to my love.)

Not surprisingly, the friction depicted in this scene rubbed off on interactions during and after filming. The silence maintained by the man in the middle of the conflict was steadfast and absolute, but the women, in ways subtle and obvious, spoken and unspoken, conveyed their distaste for each other. The stories surrounding *Silsila* are of as much, if not more, interest as the plot of the film itself. One such story is the filming of the climax.

The climax scenes were being shot at Film City. Sanjeev Kumar was caught in a fire and Rekha was to rush to rescue her on-screen husband. While the final cut did not include this scene, the original shot had Jaya holding Rekha back, pushing her away from the fire, while Amitabh went ahead to rescue Sanjeev Kumar. Just before the first take, Rekha apparently went to the cameraman and told him that she would only do one take for the scene, and no more: 'Whether you get the shot okay or not, I won't be bothered. I will be quitting the moment the first take is over.'[3]

The camera started rolling. Jaya pushed Rekha. But along with Rekha, Jaya also moved out of the frame by mistake. Rekha realized that the shot hadn't gone well but, unconcerned, she left the set. 'As the entire unit stood there stunned, Amitabh who was relaxing in his chair looked sternly at Jaya and nodded curtly, as if to ask accusingly, "So you did something?" Understanding this, Jaya, like an innocent child, said in self-defence, "I didn't do anything. I didn't say anything to her."'[4] Jaya reportedly stood there with tears in her eyes.

Cine Blitz reported another interesting incident that happened during the dubbing of the film. Rekha went to Raj Kamal Studio but before she started dubbing, she asked to be shown the songs from the film. After seeing her songs, she asked, *'Baki ke gaane kahan hain?'* (What about the other songs?) The unit members were reluctant to show Rekha Jaya's songs, but she insisted, saying, *'Unke gaane toh hum zaroor dekhenge. Uske bina to aaj* dubbing *ka mood nahi banne wala hai.'* (I will definitely see her songs. Without that, I won't be able to do the dubbing.) When she noticed that the unit members were still reluctant, she added, *'Arre bhai leke to aao. Woh to hamari rishtedar hain. Agar unka kaam nahi dekhenge to kinka dekhenge?'* (Get her songs. She is a relative. If not hers then whose work will I see?)

At this point they had to bring in the reels of Jaya's songs. As the songs were being screened, Rekha kept passing snide remarks.

Years after *Silsila*, Rekha said, 'How can anybody compare Jayaji and me when it comes to glamour? It is like Mehmood trying to be Dilip Kumar. How can you even think of it?'[5]

~

Silsila was one of the first major mainstream movies to focus on the subject of extramarital affairs. In a way, it engaged in a dialogue on love, marriage and destiny. Shobha (Jaya) is engaged to Shekhar Malhotra (Shashi Kapoor), a squadron leader with the Indian Air Force. Shekhar's brother, Amit (Amitabh Bachchan), is a playwright based in Delhi, whose heart is set on the attractive Chandni (Rekha). All is well in the lives of the couples till Shekhar dies in air combat, leaving a pregnant Shobha behind. Amit steps in as her saviour and marries Shobha. Chandni is laconically informed about the turn of events in a letter and, heartbroken, she goes on to marry Sanjeev Kumar.

Clearly, the two married couples in the film are not united by love, but by circumstances and responsibilities. Chandni and Amit are ill at ease in their respective marriages, and when fate brings them face-to-face some time later, they realize that they still love each other, and start having an affair.

However, the culmination of an extramarital affair in marriage would probably not have found the approval of audiences in India. In a Bollywood film dealing with secret liaisons and adultery, there is little hope for love to triumph. A string of events leads to a rather banal reconciliation between Amit and Shobha. Matrimony was granted supremacy over love. Traditions, morals and virtues were upheld. The movie ended up becoming a *silsila* (affair) of compromises, just like the lead actors' real lives were rumoured to be.

Silsila was released on 29 July 1981. The opening was stupendous but the momentum couldn't be sustained and it flopped, leaving everyone surprised. Yash Chopra's wife Pamela commented on this: 'Marriage is a very, very sacred institution in India, and when the director created sympathy for the two lovers who were willing to go outside their marriage and continue their love affair, he didn't carry the audience with him.'[6]

Many say the film was ahead of its time, that the audience was not ready for such a story. But ironically, according to Yash Chopra, the fault was in the selection of the cast. 'The casting went wrong. People expected the real-life story on screen. There were too many expectations,' he said after the film flopped.[7]

Rumours of affairs and scandals usually start as whispers in gossip columns, and then build into a loud media buzz before they die away, forgotten. The Amitabh–Rekha association would also have had the same fate were it not for *Silsila*. The film gave people visuals of an affair they had been imagining and talking about; it embedded the story in public memory. Till date, most media reports and features on the fabled affair are accompanied with visuals picked out from the film. *Silsila* forever embedded the Amitabh–Rekha–Jaya triangle into the public consciousness.

18

Accident

'I know people must be saying bechari Rekha, pagal hai us par, phir bhi dekho (poor Rekha, she is mad about him). Maybe I deserve that pity.' – Rekha[1]

Silsila had bombed at the box office. But a string of successes in the next twelve months saw Amitabh regain his one-man industry status. The hits included *Lawaris* (1981), *Kaalia* (1981), *Satte Pe Satta* (1982), *Desh Premee* (1982), *Namak Halal* (1982), *Khuddar* (1982) – in the latter two, Rekha was considered for the role of lead heroine) – *Desh Premee* (1982) and *Shakti* (1982). There were big flops too like *Nastik* (1982) and *Mahaan* (1982) but overall he retained his superstar status.

26 July 1982. Amitabh Bachchan was shooting a fight sequence at the Bangalore University campus for Manmohan Desai's *Coolie* (1983). The villain that Amitabh was supposed to beat up was the debutante actor

Puneet Issar, a fourth-degree black belt in martial arts. It was a simple action scene for which they had rehearsed about seven times.

Then came the actual take.

Puneet recalled it vividly. 'Amitji was much more charged. I mock punched him and threw him on the table as I was supposed to do. But Amitji took a leap, somersaulted and fell off the table.'[2] Amitabh Bachchan immediately said, *'Mujhe lag gayi hai.'* (I am hurt.) But he told Puneet, 'Relax, these things happen while shooting. It was just a mock fight.'

Amitabh got up and left. The shooting continued. Nobody realized the seriousness of the injury till the next day when it was diagnosed that Amitabh's intestines had been severely ruptured. He was operated on in Bangalore, but his condition deteriorated. By then it had hit the headlines that the nation's most-loved superstar had suffered a near-fatal accident and was critically injured. The news unleashed a mass hysteria that was unprecedented in cinematic history. The nation was traumatized. People everywhere were praying fervently for his recovery.

From Bangalore, he was transferred to the posh Breach Candy Hospital in Bombay, where, according to the actor, he went into a 'haze and coma-like situation', and was 'clinically dead for a couple of minutes'.

Amitabh was in the intensive care unit on the second floor of the hospital, connected to life support systems.

A tube was inserted in his throat and a respirator was strapped to his chest. He looked skeletally thin. But Jaya must have had no time to cry.

She left no stone unturned to ensure her husband's well-being. While tending to Amitabh's injuries, she was also praying fervently, visiting every possible place of worship: the Siddhivinayak temple, Mahim church, Haji Ali. She even attended a havan organized by the underworld don Vardarajan Mudaliyar. Jaya seemed to be in a trance; nothing mattered other than the life of her husband and fighting for his survival.

The hospital regularly released health bulletins. There were huge 'Get Well Amitabh' ads in major newspapers. Prime Minister Indira Gandhi came to see him. Her son and Amitabh's close friend, Rajiv Gandhi, was in the United States at that time but immediately returned to be by Amitabh's side. In a matter of days, the hospital's visitor book was overflowing with the names of people of national eminence who had come to pay Amitabh a visit.

The only one who wasn't allowed to see him was Rekha.

~

Rekha was allegedly barred from entering the hospital. To be denied the right to see him as he hung between life and death must have been shattering. The unfairness of the situation was overwhelming.

Reports published at that time suggested that Jaya Bachchan didn't want Rekha anywhere near her husband. Prakash Mehra recalled, 'Had Rekha asked me, I would have convinced Jaya. Here this guy was dying, *sab bhool jao* (forget everything). She is a co-star, *us rishtey se* (by virtue of that relation) [she should be allowed to see him].'[3]

According to a report published in *Movie*, Rekha decided to go to the hospital very early in the morning, without make-up, wearing a simple white cotton sari. Somehow, she managed to get permission to see him. She went up to his room, stood in the doorway for a few seconds and said a silent prayer.[4]

Later, in an explosive interview with *Filmfare*, Rekha remembered those days: 'The incident I learnt most from was the accident. What I didn't learn in 27 years, I learnt in 6 months. It made me better, stronger, and I am proud that I came out of it confident enough to conquer the world.' She expressed her agony, saying: 'Just imagine, I couldn't communicate my feelings to that person. I couldn't feel what he was going through. It was the worst kind of feeling. Even death won't be so bad. I could accept death, not this feeling of sheer helplessness, absolute helplessness.'[5]

In that phase of helplessness, Rekha too turned to God. According to reports in magazines, she organized a *jap* at Mahakaleshwar temple in Ujjain. She flew to

Tirupati and decided to cover the long uphill walk to the temple barefoot.

Amitabh Bachchan survived.

~

Released on 14 November 1983, *Coolie* became an all-time blockbuster. The film was the top grosser of 1983 and one of the biggest hits of that decade.

The careers of most people associated with the film benefited tremendously, except for Puneet Issar's. He was painted as a national villain. He recalled, 'I did not benefit from it. It was virtually a stigma. The press turned me into a life-sized monster. I never worked with Amitji again.'[6]

Puneet's agony, however, did not end there. Almost thirty-two years after the incident, Rekha appeared on the television reality show *Bigg Boss* to promote her film *Super Nani* (2014). Puneet was one of the participants on the show. While Rekha was chatty with most contestants, she completely ignored Puneet. In fact, while she greeted everyone else with a hug, when Puneet extended his arms for one, Rekha settled for a cold handshake. It could be that Rekha had never been able to forgive Puneet. Not just had he been responsible for Amitabh's injury but the accident had also precipitated a crisis from which her love wouldn't recover.

When, on the *Bigg Boss* set, Puneet told Rekha, '*Rekhaji, mujhe aapko dekh ke bahut* thoughts *aa rahe hain,*'

(Rekhaji, my mind is buzzing with thoughts seeing you), a pan-faced Rekha frostily replied that she too had 'many thoughts' swimming in her mind on seeing Puneet, hinting at the *Coolie* incident. Caught on the wrong foot, Puneet made a 'peace-out' sign and, as part of the show, started to recite a couplet: *'Jiski saza tum ho, mujhe waisa koi gunah karna hai'* (I want to commit that crime for which you are the punishment). Rekha promptly shot back, *'Aur kitne gunah karenge aap?'* (How many more crimes are you going to commit?)

~

The accident is said to have had a life-altering impact on Amitabh, Jaya and even Rekha. It is believed that the convalescence period brought Amitabh and Jaya closer. And it pushed a lone Rekha further into her solitude.

Movie reported that while Amitabh was fighting for his life in hospital, Rekha helped organize the premiere of *Umrao Jaan* (1981) and personally signed all the invitations. At the premiere, while she looked stunning in a turquoise-blue churidar kameez, her face was expressionless. The premiere was dead and 'starless'. The industry felt it was in bad taste to throw a party when Amitabh was critical. Rekha said, 'It was almost as if I were to be blamed for it, when I rightfully felt that I had to be sympathized with. I needed people to understand me, be with me, but there was no one. It was in every way the worst period in my life. I couldn't believe that the very people I'd been so nice to, gone out of my way to help, had turned against me completely.'[7]

Gossip magazines targeted Rekha for the premiere. It was insinuated that the 'Superstar' was livid and, more than Jaya, it was he who insisted that the door be shut on Rekha. Discarding her usual restraint, Jaya hinted that all was well in her married life, except that the person claiming to be the 'other woman' wasn't able to smell the coffee: 'If the man is having an affair, but is not breaking his marriage, though he says he is miserable, because his wife is so bad (and it's always the same story)…and yet, there is his home, strong and solid, and his children are doing very well, and…the family is prospering in life, everything is comfortable, he goes back home at a decent hour. Can't you rationalize for yourself, isn't it too obvious?'[8]

However, Rekha was steadfast in her claims. In her famous *Filmfare* interview, Rekha talked about Amitabh's *outward* denial of their relationship. She said, 'He did it to protect his image, his family, his children. Why should the public know of my love for him or his love for me? I love him and he loves me, that's it!'[9]

But Jaya maintained that Rekha's claims were delusions. She once said, 'Oh, yes. I've heard it time and again, about how helplessly and hopelessly in love with the married man every "other woman" is. I cannot pretend to understand or condone it. I'm never *helplessly* in love with anybody (hopelessly, yes). And there's no way I'll accept such a situation for myself or anybody I know. I believe any self-respecting human being can do it. I cannot believe that you don't want it but you're dragged into the affair in spite of yourself. How do you accept the man going home every night? Why should you degrade yourself so much and be readily available? When you don't have the man's name and are not legally accepted in any decent company, what are you getting out of this relationship? ... Does she really believe that the man comes home and twiddles his thumbs? ... Oh come on! It doesn't happen like that. And if the other woman believes that, I am sorry but she's a fool...'[10]

In her no-holds-barred interview, Rekha spoke about Jaya too: 'If you can kill your desire and stick to someone in spite of knowing that this person loves somebody else, stay under the same roof. It shows strength.' She added, 'I know, it must be terrible for his wife, but there is nothing I can do. Ye image hai na – of being a seductress and home breaker. If I had been the wife, I would have felt the same way. But I would have killed the other woman!' Rekha continued: 'No one cares what I have to say. I'm basically the other woman na? Parents are also embarrassed. Which parents will not be when their son has an affair?'[11]

This was the time that fatal cracks seemed to appear in Rekha and Amitabh's association.

Amitabh Bachchan never officially commented on this.

19

Umrao

'She was wronged. Amitabh Bachchan should have married her.' – Muzaffar Ali

Justuju jiski thi usko toh na paya hamne
Is bahaane se magar dekh li duniya hamne

The one I desired remained elusive to me
It was an excuse to witness the world's reality

According to Muzaffar Ali, 'This song from *Umrao Jaan* fits Rekha perfectly. She was wronged. Amitabh Bachchan should have married her.' Muzaffar was Rekha's director in *Umrao Jaan*, perhaps the role Rekha will be best remembered for by generations to come. While making the film, Muzaffar Ali got a close look into Rekha's life. He described her as 'a very sensitive woman'. According to him, 'She became a walking corpse. The fault is entirely

Amitabh's. He used to come and sit on our sets during the Delhi shooting of *Umrao Jaan*. That's a fact. Whenever referring to Amitabh, she always spoke using *inko, inhone*, like women do who consider themselves married. I think she considered herself married.'

Unlike many of Rekha and Amitabh's colleagues in the film industry, Muzaffar Ali was not cagey. He was direct and unequivocal: 'She is and she was in love with him. He should have definitely given her an identity. Amitabh should have married her.'

~

Muzaffar Ali cast Rekha for the lead in *Umrao Jaan* because, according to him, a 'striking feature of Rekha is that which draws from her past. Her eyes conveyed the experience of having been broken and then having pulled herself together... Life shakes up people, and if they have an artist within them, then [s]he gets more polished in the process. Rekha is a living example of this.'

For the role of Umrao, who spoke unblemished Urdu and recited poetry effortlessly, Muzaffar signed Rekha on the basis of her photographs alone. There was no customary script narration. He simply told Rekha about the role, which was challenging from an acting point of view, and that the film wasn't backed by other stars, but she said yes.

Umrao Jaan was set during the decadent 1840s when

the courtesan culture flourished at the Awadh court. Muzaffar Ali, a designer, painter and poet – an aesthete – apart from being a film director, recreated the melancholy of and nostalgia for Awadh of the mid nineteenth century, a time when Lucknawi tehzeeb, music, poetry and dance flourished. Courtesans were an intrinsic part of that cultural milieu. Rekha came to life as the courtesan Umrao Jaan in the film, based on the 1905 novel by Mirza Hadi Ruswa, *Umrao Jaan Ada*. Umrao is now etched in popular memory as Rekha.

'To praise *Umrao Jaan* is akin to lighting a lamp in the face of the blazing sun. So beautiful that fairies die with envy. A poetess so skilled that the greatest admit defeat. And a voice like a flame ablaze': with these words, Gauhar Mirza (played by Naseeruddin Shah) painted a portrait of Umrao (Rekha) for Nawab Sultan (Farooq Sheikh) in the film. And thus Rekha slipped, seamlessly, from mainstream Bollywood glamour, romance and comedy into a parallel universe of grace, elegance and intensity. Muzaffar Ali says Rekha channelled her personal emotions and pain while playing the role: 'I think Rekha became more than what I had expected of Umrao. She rose beyond the script.'

The story of *Umrao Jaan* begins in 1840. In an act of vengeance, the young Ameeran is abducted from her father's house and sold to Khanam Jaan, the owner of a brothel in Lucknow. Renamed Umrao, she is trained to become a courtesan and starts to captivate men of wealth and nobility. Umrao falls in love with Nawab Sultan

(Farooq Sheikh), but he marries another woman. She then meets and elopes with the dashing bandit chieftain Faiz Ali, who is subsequently killed by the police. Umrao tries, unsuccessfully, to flee the life of a courtesan. All around her, the old cultural environment of Awadh is crumbling and fast disappearing. Broken and disillusioned, she is left with solitude and poetry as her only companions.

~

Everyone on the sets of *Umrao Jaan* had heard about Rekha's erratic behaviour while shooting. She was said to be 'difficult to work with' and 'moody', but according to Farooq Sheikh, her conduct was a pleasant surprise: 'Despite adverse working conditions, severe winter, unmanageable crowds, and all kinds of problems, Rekha was exemplary in the manner in which she interacted with the entire unit.'[1]

Muzaffar Ali's face still lights up when he reminisces about the making of the film. The entire unit had to move from Bombay to Lucknow for shooting. According to Muzaffar, 'Rekha was a big star. So how would she disembark the train and go till the car? It would've been difficult to control the crowds on the station. I would tell her to walk exactly behind me. My height is such that if she walks exactly behind me, no one would be able to see her.'

But Rekha and Muzaffar also had their share of

conflict on certain aspects of the film. 'A film is made at many levels. On the level of music, level of lifestyle, of clothing. We faced much difficulty on the level of clothing. She carried a whole tribe of people for make-up and costume, and I did not like this,' says Muzaffar. Rekha was very conscious about her clothes and look. Before each scene, her costume team would present options in front of Muzaffar, all of which would be shot down. This was the cause of daily argument. 'They wanted to turn Rekha into a Bollywood doll. But our character was not Umrao Jaan. The character was Lucknow, and its culture. Her designer would always be standing with costumes on a hanger. That was a very big issue. I was adamant that this was not Lucknow, that she had taken the character elsewhere. They were occupied with making it *Muqaddar Ka Sikandar*,' Muzaffar Ali recounts.

As shooting progressed, the conflicts abated. Rekha realized that the film and her character's trajectory were different from all her earlier films. There would be creative discussions and critical engagement on the sets. Rekha shared her thoughts on scenes and tried to infuse the pathos of her own life into Umrao's character. 'She had realized that if she didn't listen to what we were trying to do with her, she would end up in a disaster zone,' says Muzaffar. He started involving Rekha in analyses of dialogues and music. They had regular discussions on Umrao's character and on the delicate nuances of Urdu. 'She went into that zone. It was a different world

[of] Urdu, *shayari* (poetry), tehzeeb; a huge challenge for a person from South India. In a way it was a total transformation for Rekha.'

Rekha was known for her rapid pace of dubbing in the industry. She believed she could give her performance in *Umrao Jaan* an extra edge with her skilled voice modulation, intonation and near-perfect Urdu diction. She would usually finish an entire film's dubbing in a mere three or four hours. But *Umrao Jaan*'s formidable Urdu was a challenge even for her. Muzaffar says, 'Rekha said that she'll dub it in six hours, but I wanted to get each word right, each breath right. It was not easy to dub it. She got nervous as to what was happening. Dubbing went on for a week, it took us thirty-six hours, but see her dialogue delivery in the film. She is an amazing artist.'

In an interview, Farooq Sheikh, who played Umrao's princely paramour, Nawab Sultan, revealed how he, along with Rekha and Dina Pathak, had to take a train from Delhi to Lucknow for the shoot. It was a fourteen-hour overnight journey in winter. They had been promised bedding and breakfast but once the train started, they realized that the man in charge of production had forgotten to load the bedding.

'Dinaji had a shawl but Rekhaji had only a dupatta to ward off the biting cold. It was freezing and forget about sleeping, we couldn't even sit without our teeth chattering. Yet, not a word of complaint passed through Rekhaji's lips,' he recalled.

On the return journey, they ensured that the bedding was in place but after getting off the train in Delhi, discovered that there was no car waiting for them. Her identity camouflaged by her dupatta, Rekha uncomplainingly stood beside Sheikh in the taxi queue for thirty-five minutes. As the cab whisked them away, he breathed a sigh of relief. 'Given how big a star she was then, had anyone recognized Rekhaji, she'd have been treated like a queen. But I would have surely landed in a hospital with a few broken bones for coming between her fans and their idol,' he laughed.[2]

~

Rekha won the National Award for best actress for *Umrao Jaan*. The film's art director, Manzur, music director, Khayyam, and playback singer, Asha Bhosle, also won National Awards. Given that the film did not have a large budget, it did reasonably well at the box office.

The highlight of *Umrao Jaan* was the *mujra* or courtesan dance. For the choreography, Muzaffar Ali had hired the legendary Kathak dance guru Gopi Krishna, who choreographed the magnum opus *Mughal-e-Azam* (1960), and Kumudini Lakhia, a pioneer of contemporary Kathak. According to Muzaffar, 'Rekha was comfortable with both [choreographers] but Gopi Krishna's moves came naturally to her since he was more commercial. Kumudini had nothing to do with Bollywood and brought a certain realism into the dances.' Watching the film, it is surprising to know that Rekha has no formal training in Kathak, the backbone of the movie. The courtesans of that era were all trained Kathak dancers. Muzaffar says Rekha, though untrained, had the body language and 'bhava' of a Kathak dancer.

In an interview, Rekha had said, 'Muzaffar Ali had also invited many nawabs of the bygone era, who were acquainted with the *mujra*. These nawabs were exclusively called to closely monitor my Kathak steps and many a time they guided me and came up with valuable suggestions, thus making my dance stand out.'

Over three decades later, one is haunted by the image of Umrao Jaan, her helplessness and disillusionment, her loneliness and longing, the emptiness in her eyes and her inability to escape the loveless fate of a tawaif. Umrao and Rekha fed into each other. They merged into one person.

20

Arthouse

'One doesn't grow up in a day, it takes years.' – Gulzar on Rekha

The Hindi film industry was going through a particularly bad phase in the 1980s. Its saving grace was what was referred to as parallel cinema, the Indian New Wave movement known for its serious content and neo-realism. Powerhouse actresses like Smita Patil and Shabana Azmi came to the fore during this time. With the success of Muzaffar Ali's *Umrao Jaan*, Rekha began venturing into more offbeat genres. Though *Umrao Jaan* is much celebrated, many of Rekha's other exquisite performances have gone unnoticed. Rekha forayed into arthouse films in which she worked with independent, thinking directors, mostly under Shashi Kapoor's production house. She gave terrific performances in Shyam Benegal's award-winning drama *Kalyug* (1981), and Govind Nihalani's

Vijeta (1982), Girish Karnad's *Utsav* (1985) and Gulzar's *Ijaazat* (1987).

~

Kalyug, produced by Shashi Kapoor and directed by Shyam Benegal, was the producer–director duo's second film together after the remarkable *Junoon* (1978). The basic narrative was borrowed from the Mahabharata, and the film tells the story of two rival business families that are hell bent on destroying each other.

Rekha plays Supriya, a character based on Draupadi. Raj Babbar plays Rekha's husband, who is disinterested and unaroused by his wife. Supriya yearns for her young brother-in-law, Bharatraj (played by Anant Nag). Shyam Benegal recalls, 'There is a natural courtesan grace, basically that's the kind of part she had to play.'[1] In a lingering scene towards the end of the film, Supriya takes her brother-in-law's head in her lap, while his wife sadly watches on. The critic and author Vijay Nair described her performance as 'a masterful interpretation of the modern Draupadi'.

Shyam was amused that Rekha used to act without worrying about her articulation because she knew she would be dubbing her scenes later: 'I come from a tradition where the actor is supposed to be a composite, he must do everything. I mean for one performance you don't separate the voice from the body. She came from a different tradition. She came from a tradition where verbal articulation can be separated from the performance, so you can mumble [during the shoot] and concentrate on the mime and performance rather than on the speech, unlike [in] theatre.'[2]

According to Shyam, he 'had got bookings [at a sound studio] for the whole day, from 9 in the morning to 6 in the evening, but Rekha would arrive at about 11.30 and by 1.30 she had finished all her dubbing. That too without referring to any paper. She would just watch her own scenes once and then lip read! She had that photographic memory.'[3]

Reviewing the film for *India Today*, Madhu Trehan wrote, 'It is hard to believe it is the same Rekha who swishes around in trashy films. In a scene where there is an income tax raid in her house, her bras are pulled out of her closet and fingered by inspectors; Rekha's outrage is so natural.' This scene was a metaphor for one of the most important episodes in the Mahabharata, Draupadi's *cheerharan*. Shyam Benegal masterfully captures this incident from Draupadi's point of view and Rekha's understated performance is dazzling. *Kalyug* is a film that makes you wonder why an actress of Rekha's talents chose to do numerous senseless, absurd films in her career. Rekha received critical acclaim for the film, which was also a box-office success.

~

Along with *Umrao Jaan* and *Kalyug*, Rekha was critically feted for *Baseraa* (1981), though much of her good work around that time was overshadowed by the phenomenal hype surrounding *Silsila*.

The director Ramesh Talwar's *Baseraa*, in which Rekha plays a woman who married her sister's husband after her sister became mentally ill, was a typical mainstream melodrama. It was the screenplay writer Gulzar's deft touch that made it watchable. He delicately touched on the nuances of human relationships, giving the film some really moving scenes.

But more than her performance, Ramesh Talwar remembers an incident that says a lot about Rekha's character. Ramesh had used up all the dates that Rekha had assigned to his film but some scenes were yet to be shot. Rekha had to leave for Madras to dub for another film. According to Ramesh, 'She saw my face drained of colour, and asked, "What is the matter?" I said seven scenes are still to be done and she needs to leave. I was worried [about] how it would be done, such a huge set will not be constructed again. She said, "Is this the matter? Okay. I will finish your work before leaving. Whether it finishes tonight at eight, or tomorrow night at eight, I will finish all the work."'[4]

~

Gulzar played a very important role in Rekha's career. Of the top five films that Rekha will be remembered for, at least three were touched by Gulzar: *Ghar*, *Khoobsurat* and Gulzar's masterpiece *Ijaazat*. Their connection went beyond films and when Gulzar talks about Rekha, the warmth overflows: 'As a person, she is very affectionate, and very emotional. The position she has reached cannot be attained without hard work. And one doesn't grow up in a day, it takes years.' Gulzar describes the bond that his family shares with Rekha as follows: 'We feel very proud of her. When Rakheeji still occasionally chided her, she said, "Bosky [Gulzar and Rakhee's daughter Meghna] has also grown [up], when will you, Rekha?"'[5]

Most people who have worked with Rekha at different points in her career describe her as a person full of warmth and emotion. She is seen as a girl who was mercilessly mocked for years, who suffered in solitude since childhood, who never had an equal relationship with a man, but who persevered and did not admit defeat. Many of her colleagues share a bond of love and warmth with her.

~

When Shashi Kapoor planned his magnum opus period film *Utsav*, Rekha was his first choice to play the protagonist. The acclaimed actor and playwright Girish Karnad was roped in as the director. The well-read director referred to two ancient classical Sanskrit dramas to create his screenplay: *Daridra-Charudatta* by Bhasa and *Mrcchakatika* by Sudraka. The latter, in fact, was inspired by the former, and both tell the story of the courtesan Vasantasena and her affair with the impoverished Brahman Charudatta.

The film-maker wanted to create a sensual drama against the backdrop of political turmoil. 'What I hoped to do was to revive the two qualities which ancient Indian literature had but which we seem to have lost in the course of the last one thousand years: sensuousness and humour. Not sex, but sensuousness, the poetic, tactile quality of it,' Girish Karnad said.

Much before its release, *Utsav* was all over the film media thanks to the intimate scenes that Rekha had agreed to do. It was publicized as a semi-erotic movie in which Rekha would be bolder than ever before. This was also seen as a desperate attempt by Rekha to counter the new brigade of actresses entering the industry. The hero whom the producer Shashi Kapoor selected was a debutant, Shekhar Suman. Years later, he became a household name as a television actor. Back then, as a young man, Shekhar was on cloud nine for being cast opposite Rekha.

Remembering those days, Shekhar says, 'Shashi Kapoor had selected me. But after the audition he told me that [the] final decision would be taken by Rekha. There were so many intimate scenes in the film so I think she was concerned. I was made to sit in Prithvi Theatre many times, waiting for Rekha. I would timidly keep sitting. It seemed as if a bride was sitting in wait for her groom. The groom would just not come. I kept going continuously for many days. Then, one day, she came.'[6]

Shekhar was asked to go to Shashi Kapoor's office, where Girish Karnad and Rekha were also present. Rekha said hi to him and sized him up, inspecting him closely. Shekhar was approved.

According to Shekhar, Rekha had assumed that he would be nervous and scared; the first scene that was to be shot between them was a rather intimate one. 'I remember she looked at Girish Karnad and said, "But he is a newcomer and he is supposed to be nervous but he is not. Why?" Girish answered, "Because he's been practising with a pillow the whole day." Everyone laughed and the ice was broken.'

Shekhar says Rekha 'was the most desirable woman in India. Her aura was amazing. At that time, we did not have Internet or TV, so people had a lot of curiosity to see the stars. For me, it was unbelievable that not only was she in front of me, but I was working with her as a hero. The fan and the actor in me were constantly in conflict. Then I soon steadied myself, not letting my nervousness show on my face.'

Utsav was shot at Kundapura, a small village near Mangalore. A 400-year-old house was renovated for the film and an elaborate set was constructed to recreate the ambience of the Gupta period. When the shooting started in 1984, something happened in Bombay that completely threw Rekha off. There was a massive income tax raid on her house. Shekhar recalls, 'Anyone else would have left the shooting. However, she was Shashi Kapoor's friend and she understood that such a big unit was stationed so far away, so it would lead to a huge loss. She kept on shooting without saying anything. Her house was in turmoil but she said let them do their job. I'll do mine.' This was a total turnaround from the Rekha of the 1970s who used to play truant on a whim and was disinterested in her work. Time and experience had changed her.

Rekha's sensuousness was the highlight of Utsav. Playing the role of a courtesan again, her resplendent beauty elevated each frame. But neither her performance nor the direction could match the intensity of *Umrao Jaan*. The film faltered at the level of the script and direction. The dramatic scenes appeared too theatrical and the relationships superficial. The film also failed to capture the heat and intrigue of the political saga that was simultaneously unfolding.

But the film generated enormous buzz. The premiere was held at Metro theatre in Bombay as well as in four other cities in India. Released on 26 September 1985, *Utsav* ended up a box-office disaster, despite all the hype. Not even its English version, made especially for a foreign audience, could make money. 'I incurred a loss of about Rs 1.5 crore on that. I was lucky I could pay off the debts,' Shashi Kapoor said in an interview.

Kapoor later revealed that the role he played in the film (Samsthanak) was to have been played by Amitabh Bachchan. But Amitabh had had the accident on the sets of *Coolie*, and Shashi had to step in. In an interview after the film's release, Shashi was told: 'Having watched you in that fantastic role, you can't imagine anyone else doing it.' 'But I can,' Shashi replied.

~

In the mid 1980s, when Rekha was working on these critically acclaimed films, her personal life was, as usual, constantly in the news. Strong rumours of her involvement with a succession of names made the rounds: Shailendra Singh, Kamal Haasan, the producer Rajeev Kumar, even Sanjay Dutt. One day in 1984, out of the blue, came the news that Rekha had married Sanjay Dutt; she was, in fact, only earnestly trying to help him ride through a particularly rough patch. Still, the release of the film they were doing together, *Zameen Aasmaan*, in June 1984 gained a little from these rumours. Sanjay later issued a formal denial of their alleged marriage.

Some time later, the headlines alleged that Raj Babbar and Rekha were having a romance. The press even reported a supposed fight between them at Juhu beach. Coincidentally, this was when they were working together on *Sansar* (1987).

The cycle of linking Rekha to her co-stars may have been aimed more at improving box-office collections. If at all these relationships existed, they definitely lacked the seriousness of her fixation with 'him', perhaps the only man she ever truly loved.

21

'Lady Amitabh'

*'Khoon Bhari Maang...destroyed the myth that it was
essential to have a hero as the protagonist and that heroines
were there just to serve as interludes and mannequins.'*
– M.L. Dhawan

Rekha, according to Gulzar, cannot be dismissed as
a regular mainstream song-and-dance star: *'Ghar,
Khoobsurat* and *Ijaazat,* all three films belong to distinct
genres. In all three, Rekha's performance is amazing. These
three performances tell you her range.'

Ijaazat (1987), an emotionally textured and moving
film, was based on a Bengali story, *'Jatugriha',* by
Subhodh Ghosh. Gulzar reinterpreted the story and, in
his narrative, the protagonists Sudha, played by Rekha,
and Mahendra, Sudha's husband, played by Naseeruddin
Shah, unexpectedly meet in a railway station waiting room
one stormy evening five years after Sudha had walked out

on Mahendra. Their painful past becomes the subject of a poetic conversation between them, and their story is revealed through flashbacks: Mahendra was in love with Maya (Anuradha Patel). But events unfolded in such a way that he had to marry Sudha.

Despite trying, Sudha could not ignore Maya's influence on her married life. Unable to cope, she decided to leave, freeing her husband to pursue Maya. That decision wrecked all three characters who ended up growing further apart as time passed.

Rekha gives her character heart-rending dignity. She is able to express the most complex emotions through her silence and eyes alone. *Ijaazat* was one of the highlights of her long career. *Filmfare* wrote about the film, 'One of Gulzar's most sensitive films, it also remains Rekha's most poignant performance as the possessive wife, who gives up her husband (Naseeruddin Shah) rather than share him with another woman (Anuradha Patel).'

This was the first time Rekha was cast opposite Naseeruddin Shah, already widely acclaimed for his terrific acting skills. Rekha's performance in the film was so moving that in an interview years later, when the journalist Harneet Singh asked Gulzar, 'You have etched many memorable characters. Which ones are your favourites?' Gulzar replied, 'Rekha and Naseer in *Ijaazat*.'[1]

But these were not professionally easy times for Rekha. Along with *Ijaazat*, most of her films didn't do too well at the box office despite some of them being critically lauded. These included *Zameen Aasmaan* (1984), *Faasle* (1985), *Jaal* (1986), *Pyar Ki Jeet* (1987) and *Sansar* (1987). Her star seemed to be sinking, and a younger generation of actors was snapping at her heels.

Shekhar Kapoor's *Mr India* was released the same year as *Ijaazat*, catapulting Sridevi to new heights. The next year, the director Mansoor Khan made a smashing debut with *Qayamat Se Qayamat Tak* (1988), also the debut film of both Aamir Khan and Juhi Chawla, which proved to be a musical blockbuster. Then N. Chandra's *Tezaab* (1988) gave a new language to plot lines and a successful star pair to the industry in the form of Anil Kapoor and Madhuri Dixit.

It was in 1988 that Rekha managed some sort of a comeback. It started with *Biwi Ho Toh Aisi*, which, incidentally, launched Salman Khan. Although a comedy, it had a few scenes of a genre that was dubbed by the media as 'Lady Amitabh', action sequences that had Rekha at their centre.

Also in 1988, Rekha appeared in the role of a lifetime in *Khoon Bhari Maang*. Flop-actor-turned-director Rakesh Roshan's film was a classic revenge thriller inspired by the Australian mini-series *Return to Eden* (1983). The story revolves around a wealthy, shy widow, Aarti (Rekha), who is persuaded by her friend Nandini (Sonu Walia) to marry a charmer, Sanjay Verma (Kabir Bedi). This, however, was a conspiracy to usurp Rekha's fortune after putting her out of the way, and Sanjay throws Aarti into a lake filled with crocodiles. But she survives and returns after a plastic surgery makeover to avenge the betrayal.

Rakesh Roshan intelligently marshalled Rekha's glamorous image in this 'Lady Amitabh-esque' film's narrative. She plays a plain Jane in the first half who undergoes a dramatic transformation. The film was, of course, embellished with the usual formulaic Bollywood twists.

Writing about the famous Hindi films of 1988, M.L. Dhawan of the *Tribune* said, 'With *Khoon Bhari Maang*, Rakesh Roshan destroyed the myth that it was essential to have a hero as the protagonist and that heroines were there just to serve as interludes and mannequins.' Dhawan further noted, 'This fast-paced movie was a crowning glory for Rekha, who rose like a phoenix in this remake of *Return to Eden*, and bedazzled the audience with her daredevilry. Rekha was even referred to as a "Lady Amitabh" for her brilliant action and dialogue delivery. Her performance won her [the] Filmfare best actress award. Her second after *Khoobsurat* (1980).'[2]

When the film was released, Rekha was lionized for her style, glamour and fashionable costumes. However, if you watch the film today, her clothes and get-up appear over the top, some shockingly bad. The stylist for the film seemed to have taken inspiration from the top soap operas of the time, like *Dynasty* and, of course, *Return to Eden*. There were some rather outrageous costumes and hairdos. And how can one forget the hilarious 'dance competition' between the two leading ladies, Rekha and Sonu Walia! Despite Sonu being better-looking and a better dancer, the audience was rooting for Rekha. They wanted her to win!

She did. In the film and in the industry.

Coincidentally, 1988 also saw Amitabh Bachchan make a comeback. After the assassination of Indira Gandhi, her son Rajiv became prime minister and had asked his close friend Amitabh to join politics. Amitabh contested the Lok Sabha elections from Allahabad in 1984, and won. But he soon realized that he wasn't cut out for the job. Fed up with politics and the scandal surrounding him after the Bofors scam, he resigned from the Allahabad seat. His films had been boycotted by his political opponents, but then came the release of Tinnu Anand's *Shahenshah* (1988). The film opened to pathetic reviews and was declared a flop at many places, but in terms of box-office collections, it was the second biggest film of the year.

Rekha had braved many storms to get where she was. But she couldn't have guessed that there were many more storms, harder challenges, right around the corner.

22

Suicide

'Nobody said a word. Except Shashi Kapoor. He sent me a condolence note.' – Rekha

With the success of *Khoon Bhari Maang*, Rekha decided to pursue the action-heroine formula. But the 1989 *Kasam Suhaag Ki*, starring Rekha and Dharmendra, tanked even though it was a cocktail of Rekha's signature avatars, a courtesan in a revenge drama. Next came Manoj Kumar's *Clerk*, also a box-office disaster, though it now enjoys an afterlife as a so-bad-that-it's-good cult favourite. Even Saawan Kumar, who had helped Rajesh Khanna make a comeback in *Souten* (1983), wasn't able to reverse Rekha's losing streak with *Souten Ki Beti* (1989).

Rekha, then in her mid thirties, had clearly aged, and couldn't quite hope to compete with the new cohort of younger actresses that included Sridevi, Meenakshi Seshadri and Juhi Chawla. Even the *Sholay* director

Ramesh Sippy's *Bhrashtachar* (1989), in which Rekha, cast opposite the reigning superstar Mithun Chakraborty, plays an intrepid journalist, bombed.

Rekha's career was sputtering, younger actresses were fast overtaking her and the rumour mill about the 'Superstar' and her had gone silent. It was under these circumstances that Rekha married the Delhi businessman Mukesh Agarwal on 4 March 1990, and elbowed her way back into the headlines.

But even *Bahurani* (1990), released right after her marriage to Mukesh and the attendant media hysteria, flopped. Of course, all the blame can't be placed at Rekha's door – the film had a hackneyed plot – but the writing on the wall was clear: Rekha's stardom was waning and even her much-talked-about wedding wasn't enough to draw audiences into theatres.

~

Rekha and Mukesh's honeymoon period was short and the marriage disintegrated within months. Rekha was back in Bombay from Delhi, desperately trying to salvage a career that was going nowhere. While she was in New York for a stage show came the final blow: in October 1990, seven months after their hurried wedding, Mukesh committed suicide.

Along with the film industry, it was as if every drawing room in the country wanted an answer from Rekha. People close to Mukesh, and even those who had never known him, were unanimous in their accusation: Rekha was somehow responsible for the suicide. That Rekha didn't immediately deploy a PR team to refute the allegations worked against her, for silence is often taken to be a sign of guilt. Instead, Rekha went underground. It didn't matter whether Rekha did this out of guilt or grief, the facts were now irrelevant. Rekha was the target of a vicious national witch hunt.

About those days, Rekha said, 'Nobody said a word. Except Shashi Kapoor. He sent me a condolence note. (Earlier) Shashi was the first to congratulate me when I got married, saying, "I owe you a party. You have worked in our films, so you are a part of our family. Send me a guest list." But I never could.'[1]

Finally, in December 1990, Rekha cleared the air and presented her version of events in *Filmfare*. In an interview titled 'I Didn't Kill Mukesh', Rekha said that she wanted the people who matter to her, her fans, her relatives, to know the truth.

She said, 'The divorce was not my idea in the first place. It was Mukesh who broached it first. I had begun to sense the vast differences in our outlook and temperament... during our brief honeymoon in London. Maybe it was wrong on my part to have rushed into an arranged marriage. Even then I didn't want to give up, having openly expressed my desire to make a success of the marriage. Not that there is anything wrong in two people parting ways if they find they are incompatible. I am not the kind to sustain [a] bad marriage under false pretenses. But my attitude was very positive, and I was determined to succeed. I should have known that it takes two people to make a marriage work… A stage came in our relationship when both of us decided that our incompatibility was too much to overcome and that we should part as friends. As evident from the divorce papers, the decision was to separate by mutual consent. There was absolutely no reason for anybody to hide the divorce papers from Mukesh since he was party to it.'

It was widely reported that Mukesh had hanged himself with Rekha's dupatta; this was taken to be symbolic of the fact that it was Rekha's alleged betrayal of Mukesh that prompted him to commit suicide. Rekha rebutted this construction: 'How did they come to the conclusion that it was my *dupatta* [that he hanged himself with]? Was my name written on it? It looks as if they are desperate to prove that I "killed" Mukesh.'[2]

∼

Mukesh's family and friends were unanimous in blaming Farzana, Rekha's secretary, for this tragedy. Everyone in the industry knows that Farzana stays by Rekha's side like a shadow. It is common knowledge that it is not possible to reach Rekha without going through Farzana, the gatekeeper, first. Mukesh's sister-in-law bitterly remarked,

'Initially her [Rekha's] whole family came on a holiday [to Delhi]: Radha, Dhanno [Rekha's sisters] and Teju [Rekha's brother-in-law]. We had such a good time with them. But whenever she started coming with Farzana, her secretary, there was a total change in her behaviour.' She further alleged, *'Un dono ke beech mein alag hi* behaviour *chal raha tha* (They behaved unusually with each other). Friends are different, sisters are different; this was not like that.'[3] Mukesh's brother, Anil Gupta, added, 'Their relationship was not normal. Even Mukesh could see that. He would literally receive instructions from Farzana, and which husband can take that? When he tried to put his foot down with Rekha about Farzana, Rekha would get into [a] terrible temper and walk out. Do you call that normal?'[4]

'How can I tell you in plainer words?' said Mukesh's sister-in-law. 'She and Rekha behaved like husband and wife. I've seen it with my own eyes. If only he had never met Rekha, Mukesh would be still alive today.'[5]

Mukesh's suicide note clearly said that no one should be blamed for his death. He also wrote that he wanted his brother Anil to look after his close friend Akash Bajaj and her two children. The note stated that he was not leaving anything to his wife Rekha, as she was quite wealthy in her own right. Anil Gupta said, 'If there are stories going around that Rekha wanted Mukesh's money and property, let me tell you that is not true. She never asked for a thing from us.'[6]

Mukesh's friend and former police commissioner of Delhi Neeraj Kumar adds, 'I remember that Rekha never staked any claims to anything. I also remember that Mukesh's brother told me that there had been a very expensive camera that Mukesh owned. In those days, it was something of a novelty to have an automatic camera. So they said that perhaps she had kept the camera. Maybe… as a memory of the relationship.'[7] A camera in which, perhaps, their few beautiful moments had been captured.

Years later, remembering that dark phase, Rekha told Simi Garewal, 'It wasn't love, that's for sure. Before anything registered, it was all over but then sometimes that one small thing can have a profound effect on your life. That was the time I really really grew up. I became a woman of the world.'[8]

~

After staying underground for two months, Rekha made her first public appearance at the producer-director Sultan Ahmed's party, dressed in black. She is said to have greeted everyone present at the party with a smile. She seemed unsure and was reportedly working on restoring her self-confidence, and some sanity in her life. Rekha had next to no films in hand and had been shunned by the industry. But at this party, all the Bollywood insiders who had been vowing never to work with her came forward eagerly to chat. No one looked the other way; no one left the party because of her. This was a good sign.

Rekha decided to start afresh, once again.

~

Before Mukesh's death, Rekha had been signed by K.C. Bokadia for *Bharat Ki Nari*. Bokadia perhaps felt that a film with such a title wouldn't work after the scandal Rekha was emerging from. But he decided to take the gamble anyway.

When Rekha went for the first shoot of the film, she offered to step down. Bokadia firmly declined her offer.

After reworking the storyline, the film's name was changed to *Phool Bane Angaray*. The film revolves around Rekha, whose on-screen husband, a police officer, is murdered by a corrupt politician. To add to that, Rekha's character is raped. The plot revolves around how Rekha gets sweet revenge.

On the first day of the shoot, before Rekha came in, thousands had thronged to see her. The media was present as well. Rekha saw the crowds from behind the tinted windows of her car. How would everyone react upon seeing her?

After months of being a recluse, she gathered courage and stepped out. As soon as the crowd saw her, they screamed with joy. Chants of 'Rekha! Rekha!' filled the air. People were going crazy for just one glimpse of her.

Rekha broke into a smile. People were excitedly waving at her. Rekha waved back. Her face was glowing with happiness.

This incident was widely reported, and other positive news from the shooting of *Phool Bane Angaray* was also published regularly. The film got a lot of publicity. The film journalist Prem Panicker, who had gone to cover the shooting, managed to talk to Rekha. Panicker recalled, 'It is strange how few men and women look you in the eyes all the time they are talking; Rekha holds your eyes throughout, and the effect is, in a weird way, mesmeric.'

This mesmeric effect was evident on screen. Rekha carried the film on her shoulders. Prem Chopra, who played the main villain in the film, recalled, 'You have to give the credit of this film only to her. This was her comeback vehicle after the tragedy and she was fighting with her back against the wall. When you're in such a situation, you give your best.' *Phool Bane Angaray*, released eight months after Mukesh's death, was a superhit. Viewers lined up outside cinema halls to watch the film with a female 'hero' in the lead role.

23

Orphaned

'Most of the times I was mother to my mother and to my siblings.' – Rekha

Phool Bane Angarey catapulted Rekha back into the news. But there was something different about this Rekha. According to Prem Panicker, who interviewed Rekha during the shooting of *Phool Bane Angarey*, 'She came over, sat down, and said "Hello" and "No personal questions, please; I will talk of the film, but nothing more", all in one breath.'[1] Gone was the 'media darling' who never gave a moment's thought before opening up to the press. Gone was the no-holds-barred actress who never shied away from making blunt headline-worthy remarks.

But Panicker persisted and asked her how she was managing to bounce back after the tragedy. She told him that she had never had an entirely happy relationship with anyone; not with her father or her mother or her sisters or any man in her life. There had, Rekha said, always been both happiness and hurt. And when that happens, consistently over time, you learn to put up inner defences to shield yourself from pain, she said.

~

Rekha's mother Pushpavalli passed away in Madras after a prolonged illness in 1991.

Rekha had faced many ups and downs in her life, but her mother stood by her through them all. Pushpavalli had worked hard to see her daughter achieve success. She had been ill for a few years before she died and had spent much time in Madras. But, till Pushpavalli's death, Rekha had the security of knowing that her mother was around. Rekha's bungalow is testament to the closeness shared by mother and daughter: Rekha had named it Pushpavalli. Now that reassuring presence was gone. After Pushpavalli's death, the emptiness and solitude in Rekha's life got amplified.

After Mukesh and Pushpavalli died, Rekha became a recluse. She minimized her interactions with the outside world. She gave fewer interviews, and even in those one saw a significantly toned-down Rekha. She no longer made sensational statements, rather, she became melancholic, almost philosophical. She would allude to 'him', but no names would be taken. This tumultuous phase of her life completely transformed Rekha.

~

Till her dying breath, Rekha's mother did not get validation for her relationship with Rekha's father, Gemini Ganesan. However, in 1994, when Filmfare decided to honour Gemini with a lifetime achievement award, Rekha was invited to present it to him.

At a huge function in Madras, Rekha touched her father's feet in front of everyone, and gave him his award. Gemini said that he was happy to receive the award from his 'dear child from Bombay'. Her entire childhood had been spent without her father. That he never accepted them publicly was a wound that stayed with Rekha and Pushpavalli. However, that day, Rekha seemed happy and moved by the thawing of relations. She said, 'It is the proudest moment in my life to share the same dais as my father and present him the award.'

Gemini had finally publicly acknowledged Rekha as his daughter in front of the entire film industry but, sadly, Pushpavalli wasn't around to see it.

~

According to the actor Tej Sapru, who is married to Rekha's youngest sister, Dhanalakshmi, Rekha was something of a lone warrior: 'All the sisters loved their mother very much but Rekha was special because she had really fought. *Rekha ne sab kuch akele hi kiya.* [She did everything on her own.] Her fight was tremendous. In fact, she did a lot of things to take the family to a certain level.'[2]

Rekha blindly signed multiple films in the 1970s and 1980s because she had to take care of her large family: two brothers, three sisters and, of course, her mother. The more films she signed, the more she earned. There used to be a huge disparity between the pay of lead actors and actresses. Actresses were usually assigned shorter roles and didn't have a central place in the film so they didn't take as much time to complete a project as the lead actor, or earn as much.

Rekha herself talked about her responsibilities to her family. 'Most of the times I was mother to my mother and to my siblings. The mother instinct in me was too strong from the time I was born…and has been overflowing all my life. But then again I guess it's a woman's prerogative to feel this way. Some people are marked for life. I was a breadwinner. I had to grow up overnight and take care of my siblings. My brother died prematurely, I had seen so many siblings of co-stars hooked on to alcohol, drugs. I promised myself long ago that I'd preserve myself.'[3]

According to Tej, 'As a sister, she [Rekha] is excellent. There was a phase when no one else worked in her family. She was the only person running the house. She was working and she made them study, and in [the] case of Radha, the entire responsibility of her wedding was shouldered by her [Rekha].'

According to the journalist and author Bharathi S. Pradhan, Rekha single-handedly nurtured her family, financially and emotionally. She was a pillar of strength for her siblings when their mother was unwell. She made sure that her sisters never had to go through the financial difficulties and turmoil that she went through at a very young age.

This sense of sacrifice and duty reflects in Rekha's choice of films. In films like *Suhaag* (1979) and *Muqaddar Ka Sikandar* (1978), for instance, she portrayed characters who were forced to adopt the vocation of a tawaif for the sake of their families.

According to Jerry Pinto, Rekha agreed to do certain 'really low-budget, silly film[s]' because they were based on the themes of sacrifice and abandonment, which must have appealed to her. Pinto singled out *Jeevan Dhaara* (1982) as an example. In the film, Rekha plays the part of Raj Babbar's secretary who is responsible for the upkeep of her family. Raj Babbar falls in love with her, and wants to get married but Rekha is unsure because she has to take care of her family. Raj promises to do this but on the day of their wedding, Rekha's brother who was involved with the underworld is beaten to death, and Rekha calls off the wedding because she feels responsible for her brother's orphaned children. According to Pinto this didn't seem 'particularly convincing'. There was no reason, he said, that

Raj couldn't help take care of the children. Pinto sums it up by saying, 'The only reason she could have done it [*Jeevan Dhaara*] is because she wanted to play out the fantasy of abandonment.'[4] Her penchant for playing the courtesan couldn't have, according to Pinto, been good for her career.

24

Afterlife

'I would like to ask...[the media] whether they have actually seen me doing something immoral, doing something unacceptable with the concerned lady.' – Amitabh Bachchan

In the 1990s, Rekha's contemporaries like Rakhee and Hema Malini had started to do 'character roles'; they played second fiddle to the lead heroines and accepted parts like those of the hero's sister or mother. Rekha, on the other hand, was still signing films that had her in a lead role. After *Khoon Bhari Maang* and *Phool Bane Angaray*, Rekha went on to sign many more revenge thrillers. All these films had Rekha at the centre of the plot. But according to Jerry Pinto, 'It's very dangerous for female film stars to get too big. So almost all of them will give one interview at one point in their lives when they say I want to do "heroine-oriented roles" from now on. This is the beginning of their end. Because you can name on your fingers the "heroine-oriented roles" that have actually been Bollywood successes... There is one *Mother India* [1957], there is one *Damini* [1993], there is one *Noorie* [1979], they come in bursts... And then it goes back to being dominated by men... This desire to work in "meaningful" films, to do good films, is the beginning of the end.'

It was indeed the beginning of the end for Rekha, then in her early forties. Her films *Insaf Ki Devi* (1992), *Geetanjali* (1993) and *Madam X* (1994) – the latter two saw her in a double role – *Ab Insaaf Hoga* (1995) and *Udaan* (1997) were hopeless flops.

As a heroine, Rekha's career had ended. But what she did next is something that no actress before or after Rekha has managed.

~

When her films failed to get noticed, Rekha decided to make a statement through extravagant and narcissistic photoshoots. Her relationship with the camera was perfect. 'Rekha is the first one who started the personalized theme-based photoshoot fad in Bollywood. The camera loves her and she loves the camera,' says the fashion photographer Jayesh Sheth. According to Sheth, Rekha loved experimenting with her look. She used to do her own hair, make-up and costumes for the shoots. Even fully clothed, she was able to 'generate the kind of sensuality which is so rare in today's times'.

Gautam Rajadhyaksha, who took some stunning photographs of Rekha, once said, 'Rekha is India's ultimate cover girl. She is extremely hard-working, and takes a lot of pain over every single picture. No photograph of hers is a mistake. I think stars like her, who take so much trouble to be in the public eye, deserve to be loved and treated like legends.'[1] And that is where she was headed.

According to Sheth, who worked with Rekha for twelve years, they did a shoot practically every month. Rekha became obsessed with her images. And went on to do many controversial photoshoots, including a nude one with the actress Kajol, in which they are seen sharing a towel. The 1990s saw Rekha more on the covers of magazines than on the big screen.

Pinto sums it up: 'She started by being a starlet, she went on to being a star, she then became an actor, a genuine actor and then she became a diva.'

~

The mid 1990s saw three notable films that fed off Rekha's 'diva' image. In Umesh Mehra's *Khiladiyon Ka Khiladi* (1996), Rekha plays a desirable vamp who seduces the young hero, Akshay Kumar. They shot a sizzling song sequence, 'In the Night No Control', in which Rekha and Akshay cavort in some sort of a mud bath. Rumours of an affair between them helped further her sexy-at-forty image. Rekha won a Filmfare award for best supporting actress for that role.

The other two memorable films of this phase were Mira Nair's *Kama Sutra* (1996), in which Rekha plays the role of a Kama Sutra instructor, and Basu Bhattacharya's swan song *Aastha* (1997), in which she plays a bored housewife who became a prostitute. Both films are known for their explicit love scenes.

While much was written about Rekha and she was photographed endlessly, her interviews became rarer and rarer. According to the journalist, screenwriter and director Khalid Mohamed, who had been close to Rekha, the mystique and enigma that Rekha cultivated was 'put on'. Rekha was essentially unchanged, but she chose to project a different image. This new image was sustained by carefully planned and limited media exposure.[2]

~

After mega flops like *Qila* (1998) and Saawan Kumar's *Mother* (1999), Rekha gave a graceful performance in Shyam Benegal's *Zubeidaa* (2001). In 2001 Rekha got a Filmfare lifetime achievement award. She came on stage with at least four sheets of paper with the names of people who had contributed immensely to her career. She read sweet thank-you messages for many film-makers, dance directors, even friends. But one name was missing from the thank-you list: Amitabh Bachchan.

~

Over the years, Rekha had given countless interviews in which she took Amitabh's name and unequivocally said she was in a relationship with him. While most of these may get buried in archives under reams of yellowing paper, one interview will stand out for posterity: her appearance on the TV show *Rendezvous with Simi Garewal* in 2004.

Dressed in a cream sari and wearing a chunky gold necklace, Rekha changed her tune on her association with Amitabh on that show. When asked if she fell in love with Amitabh while making the ten films that they acted in together, she said, 'Absolutely. Duh, that's a dumb question. I have yet to come across a single man, woman, child who can help but fall completely, passionately, insanely, desperately, hopelessly in love with him. So why should I be singled out? What do I deny? I'm not in love with him? Of course I am. *Duniya bhar ka love aap le lejiyega* [take all the love there is in the world] and add some more, I feel that for that person. Bottom line.'

But then, much to everyone's surprise, Rekha flatly denied ever being involved with him. She said, 'You want to know the truth? This is headline, okay? There was never a personal connection with him, that's the truth.

Never ever. There was no truth to the controversies and speculation,' she told Simi. This seemed to be a well-rehearsed Rekha, with her guard up. She turned the story on its head: she admitted that she was fascinated by and in love with Amitabh; but more in the nature of a smitten fan, not a paramour.

At the end of the show, she hummed the song '*Yeh Kahaan Aa Gaye Hum*' from *Silsila*, and said again that while she did love Amitabh, they never had a romantic relationship. This was a new Rekha. In earlier interviews, she played the wounded lover. Now, she spoke of a higher kind of love. Her new Meera avatar was hard to swallow.

~

Rekha's interview was in sync with Amitabh Bachchan's interview[3] to Simi in 1998. In that interview, Amitabh spoke in detail about his alleged relationship with Rekha for the first time:

> **Simi:** One rumour that comes up like a virus every few years is your link-up with Rekha. Why does that happen? What generates it?
> **Amitabh:** Ask the people who generate it.
> **Simi:** Who generates it?
> **Amitabh:** The media.
> **Simi:** Is it just the media, you feel?

Amitabh: Well, if there is somebody else then I must be made aware of it.

Simi: Do you ever meet each other?

Amitabh: She has been my co-star and colleague and when we were working together obviously we met each other. Socially, we have nothing in common. That's about it.

Simi: You haven't met each other since…?

Amitabh: Years. I mean sometimes we bump into each other at a function…an award function, for example, or at a social gathering, but that's about it.

Simi: But there's been no interaction since you stopped working together?

Amitabh: No, we haven't worked [together] for donkey's years.

Simi: And there is no social interaction?

Amitabh: No, not at all.

Simi: Do these rumours bother you?

Amitabh: No. I face these accusations month after month, but quite honestly some of the more recent accusations have been rather ridiculous. There were claims that I had moved in with her, in her house, and that she'd moved into my house, and they had photographs of that house where I'd been keeping her, so to say, which is just a big joke. That house is mine, my family stays there, my ailing parents live there, I look after them. I think it's terribly insensitive of the media to post these accusations over me without any kind of verification, without any kind of truth. I would like to ask some of them whether they have actually seen me doing something immoral, doing something unacceptable with the concerned lady. I would like to ask them when was it that you saw the two of us together, which gave an impression to you of any kind of link-up?

'The concerned lady' and Amitabh were finally on the same page.

25

Rajya Sabha

'Rekha is one person who detested politics so much that she had stopped reading daily newspapers.' – Rasheed Kidwai

The new millennium saw Rekha, who turned fifty in 2004, take up some small but special and, critically, age-appropriate, roles: in Raj Kumar Santoshi's *Lajja* (2001), Ram Gopal Varma's *Bhoot* (2003) and Rakesh Roshan's *Krrish* trilogy (2006). With able directors, Rekha has always managed to act brilliantly. But, in typical Rekha fashion, there have also been a bunch of B-grade comedies that didn't really deserve her energy or attention: *Bachke Rehna Re Baba* (2005), *Kudiyon Ka Hai Zamana* (2006) and *Super Nani* (2014). Rekha even did an 'item number' in *Parineeta* (2005); wearing a glittering red net sari, rose in hair, she danced to '*Kaisi Paheli Zindagani*', perhaps her last appearance as a 'nautch girl', so to speak. She had the audience eating out of her hands.

Interestingly, post 2002, award ceremonies have become a ritual of sorts in the otherwise reticent Rekha's life. Each year, she comes on stage at a few functions to give away the best actor or best actress award. Many wonder why she is given this important opportunity year after year.

At these functions, when Rekha is on stage, the camera invariably zooms in on Amitabh Bachchan, and vice versa. This has become somewhat of an event, a national rite, to look forward to. It speaks volumes about the nation's fascination with their alleged affair. So what if they both now deny the relationship? None of Rekha's television appearances are complete without an indirect reference to 'him': whether through jokes or even just singing Amitabh songs. For her part, Rekha has embraced the eternal Meera image.

In 2009, Amitabh and Rekha made headlines, again, for their association. The occasion was the fifty-fourth Filmfare awards function. Amitabh had arrived with his son, Abhishek, and daughter-in-law, Aishwarya. Just then, Rekha came over and seemed to exchange pleasantries with Abhishek and Aishwarya. But Amitabh was seen looking the other way and then walking off post-haste. Captured on camera, the visuals were splashed all over television and print. An old obsession had been revived. Everyone wanted to know why Amitabh 'ran away' from Rekha.

According to Sushmita Dasgupta, author of *Amitabh: The Making of a Superstar* (2006), she always believed

Amitabh when he repudiated his alleged affair with Rekha. But when he 'suddenly got up and moved away' as Rekha approached him, Dasgupta changed her mind: 'This makes me believe that, yes, they did have an affair. The sudden getting up and moving away was a giveaway… Why would a man want to do that if he is not guilty of something?'

Amar Singh, a Samajwadi Party politician who was once extremely close to the Bachchans, narrated another incident: 'Once, Shabana Azmi invited us for her birthday. I reached her house along with Jaya and Amitabh. We reached on time, and Amitabh told his driver to go eat since they would take long. Upon reaching inside, we saw Rekha was already present there. As soon as Amitji saw Rekha, he immediately returned outside. The driver had gone to eat food, so we hailed a taxi, hastily boarded it, and returned home.' According to Amar Singh, neither did Amitabh ever bring up this incident nor did Amar Singh prod him on it. But Amar Singh says, 'This hints that there was some relationship… If there was no relationship, he could have at least wished Shabanaji, and indulged in a cordial conversation with Rekha.'[1]

According to Amar Singh, 'Once a sympathetic Hemaji talked to me about Rekha's feelings. She told me that you consider Amitabh your brother. Rekha is my friend. Why don't you do something?' But Amar Singh said he did not want to get involved in people's private affairs.

Soon enough the aftershocks of the Amitabh–Rekha scandal would reach the House of Elders in New Delhi.

~

In 2012, the Congress nominated Rekha to the Rajya Sabha. This was surprising given that Rekha had never showed any inclination towards politics or social service. Most actors who had entered politics, like Shabana Azmi, Nargis or Prithviraj Kapoor, had a proclivity towards politics or showed some interest in social work. Rasheed Kidwai, Sonia Gandhi's biographer and senior journalist, says, 'Rekha is one person who detested politics so much that she had stopped reading daily newspapers. She had once remarked, "I do not wish to see ugly lungs of politicians."'

According to Kidwai, the politics of nominating Rekha to the Rajya Sabha should be easy to understand. It is similar to the circumstances under which Rajesh Khanna had been invited into politics by the Congress following the souring of the Gandhis' relationship with Amitabh. Now Rekha had been pitted against Jaya, apparently also as a response to Jaya's personal views on the Gandhis.

Jaya, herself a Rajya Sabha member, was present at the Upper House on 15 May 2012 when Rekha was to take oath of office. While Rekha was taking the oath, the cameras kept zooming in on Jaya's face. This left a bad taste in Jaya's mouth and it was reported that she voiced her displeasure openly.

Jaya's chagrin at Rekha's arrival was palpable. She asked that her seat be changed from number ninety-one, perhaps too close for comfort to Rekha's number ninety-nine, to seat number 143.

A changed Rekha no longer comments on such things. She has made only a few staid and uneventful appearances at the Rajya Sabha, and has been criticized for not taking her role more seriously and her abysmally low attendance in Parliament, about 6 per cent.

26

Farzana

'She and Rekha behaved like husband and wife.'
– Mrs Anil Gupta

When the renowned sufi singer from Pakistan Abida Parveen was once invited by the columnist Malavika Sangghvi to sing at her Bombay residence, the legendary singer requested that Rekha be invited too. 'If there is anyone who knows and appreciates my music, it is Rekha,' the singer reportedly said to Sangghvi. Throughout that evening, it was as if Parveen was singing only to Rekha, only for her. And Rekha was one of the few who knew every verse, every tune of her repertoire. This story is one of the many folklores that contribute to the mystique of Rekha.

According to Sangghvi, 'Like most successful single women who live on their own, Rekha has the time and freedom to pursue her interests and take care of herself.

And she puts her time to good use... She is preternaturally refined. Form, fragrance, tone, colour, texture – Rekha takes it all in... She discovered Ayurveda, yoga, rituals and indigenous customs long before they were current. Her business is herself, and she tends to it extraordinarily well.'[1]

Rekha admits that she can hardly recognize herself when she watches her old films, from before her dramatic makeover. 'In my case it has been a complete transformation. My thinking, my expression...everything has changed. Little, little things, like how I react to love, to anger or to [a] funny situation. My gestures...my movement are different now. In fact, I don't remember much about those years.'[2] As mentioned earlier, Rekha considered *Muqaddar Ka Sikandar* to be a kind of break-point in her life, a 'period of self-discovery'. Her partiality to such roles became evident over time. Indeed, Rekha performed the role of a courtesan or the 'other woman' on dozens of occasions. In more than thirty films to be precise. In many films, she appears on screen just to perform a single song as a nautch girl.

Khalid Mohamed observed that in most of Rekha's celebrated work, including in *Umrao Jaan* and as Zohrabai in *Muqaddar Ka Sikandar*, she played the role of a courtesan who is basically an outsider. If there is one exemplar for such roles in the Hindi film industry it is Meena Kumari. Rekha must have been moved and inspired by that most famous of Bollywood nautch girls on whom she modelled herself. She even hired Meena

Kumari's famous make-up man after her demise. Dinesh Raheja, former editor of *Movie*, who has interviewed Rekha several times, recounted an interesting anecdote about Rekha's affection for Meena Kumari: Rekha used to frequent Meena Kumari's house, and so did her friend Yogita Bali. During one such visit, Rekha asked Meena Kumari, 'Meenaji, I am very curious to know, do you like Yogita Bali more or me more?' Meena Kumari's response to this was: '*Yogita hain na, woh meethi hain, aur tum ho na, namkeen ho. Aur namkeen ka zayka hamesha zyada der yaad rehta hai.*[3] (Yogita is sweet and you are savoury; and savoury things have a longer aftertaste.)

The Hollywood legend Sophia Loren was another of Rekha's idols. Both women have a lot in common: they both underwent dramatic physical transformations, had to overcome language barriers in the film industry and became sex symbols and pin-ups. Despite their glamour and fame, both remained essentially true to their roots: Loren continued to do Italian films and never gave up her girl-from-Naples accent. Rekha has never abandoned her Kanjeevaram sari, gold jewellery and mogra-in-hair look. Both were obsessed with certain men, obsessions that led to their own transformations. If Carlo Ponti discovered the subtle Sophia Loren, Rekha has unabashedly declared that Amitabh Bachchan was the inspiration behind her metamorphosis and life's work.

Whatever be the truth behind their alleged affair, no one is ever able to think of Rekha without thinking of

Amitabh Bachchan. According to Amitabh Bachchan's biographer Sushmita Dasgupta, 'I believe Amitabh knew from day one that he wasn't serious about Rekha. Also, he's very, very class conscious... Rekha was perhaps an ego trip.'[4]

She elaborates, 'As Amitabh moved away from the Hrishikesh Mukherjee school of filmmaking, Jaya was upset with his choice of films and at the way he was slowly becoming self-involved. He would often fall silent with her while opening up with the rest of the world. Gregarious and conversational with his writers and directors, Amitabh hardly spoke in her presence.' The new kind of film that Amitabh was doing meant that he had to be paired opposite a different kind of co-star. Rekha fit the bill perfectly, and she was happy to play the swooning love interest. According to Dasgupta, the contast between *Do Anjaane* and *Khoon Pasina* best illuminates the change. In *Do Anjaane*, the director Dulal Guha wasn't attempting to channel Amitabh's stardom for the movie. As a result, 'Rekha emerged as a powerful, wilful woman'. But in *Khoon Pasina*, where Amitabh, the superhero, looms large, Rekha is reduced to 'a prop'. And as Amitabh's stature grew, all his lead actresses were reduced to just that: props.

When their association began, Rekha shed the image of a crass sex siren and became elegant, stylish and dignified. But the films for which Rekha is best known, and that mark her as a genuinely talented actress, are the ones that don't have Amitabh in them. Over time, people saw in

Rekha the feminine avatar of Amitabh. In fact, the way she carried herself in films like *Khoobsurat*, *Umrao Jaan* and *Phool Bane Angaray*, and her voice modulation in them, strongly echo the influence of Amitabh Bachchan.

It is often said that even her secretary and aide, Farzana, has been cast in the image of Amitabh.

∼

Malavika Sangghvi described Farzana as a 'waif-like androgynous person'. Farzana usually wears trousers and a button-down shirt with a tailored jacket. She wears her hair short, in a style oddly reminiscent of Amitabh. Sangghvi says that anyone who knows Rekha knows that half of her success and mystique is to the credit of Farzana, Rekha's lifelong friend and dedicated secretary. Farzana serves as Rekha's eyes and ears, adviser and aide, buffer and shield, confidante and conspirator in all her pursuits and interests. Without her, Rekha would be lost. Sangghvi wrote, once when Rekha and Farzana were in a car with the window rolled down at a red light, 'a pesky urchin was beginning to grate with his antics. But Rekha, who sat near the window, did not, she could not, react with irritation. After all, she was the legend; how could she? But I noticed, before the situation got out of hand, without being asked, as if she knew her boss's mind even before she knew her own, Farzana reached across and rolled the window up. Through it all Rekha sat still, the smiling legend with no dent in her image. That's what a good secretary's for.'[5]

But theirs surely isn't a one-way relationship. Rekha values Farzana's presence in her life. Sangghvi revealed that once a hostess who had them over for dinner exclaimed that Rekha refused to eat before Farzana did. Rekha once told Sangghvi about what an intellectual her aide was: 'She reads the papers every morning.' In fact, in Rekha's interview with Simi Garewal, she said that she had never read a book in her life but knows many by heart, all because Farzana reads to her every day.

It has even been suggested that Rekha is in a 'relationship' with Farzana that goes beyond the professional. This first came up after Mukesh's death when there were rumours that Rekha is bisexual. Rekha retaliated to these rumours and came out in support of Farzana: 'All that has been said about our relationship is the fabrication of sick minds.'[6]

According to Jerry Pinto, 'For a lot of film stars, a lot of female film stars who were brutalized by men, relationships with other women were often gentle, soothing, nurturing, and I think Farzana was then kind of made into Amitabh. So if you look at her pictures where she is wearing broad coats and she's got a similar hairstyle like Amitabh Bachchan, which is like bizarre. Very strange but who else will you get to do that? Who else will allow you to reinvent them in the shape and likeness of your alleged boyfriend?'[7]

~

Rekha's relationship with Amitabh was probably the single biggest influence in her life. In her own words, 'Whatever has happened in my life, the growth, the vitamins, the pep, everything comes from him. But marriage? Why should you think of the impossible and be unhappy?'[8]

In some ways it seems that Rekha didn't really want her most ardent wish to come true. Once in an interview, she made it clear that even if her lover decided to leave his wife, she won't marry him. 'I know the day he walks out on his wife, I will lose all respect for him. If he can do that to her who has given up everything for him, it would be easier for him to walk out on me. That is why I don't want to marry him. I will never marry him even if he asks me.'[9]

Rekha and Amitabh have fascinated the nation with their alleged affair for the last four decades. The Fred Astaire and Ginger Rogers partnership throws up a parallel here: 'He gave her class and she gave him sex appeal.'

When he became a legend, she carved out a lifelong role for herself as a *jogan*. Rekha is now firmly ensconced in her own legend. Her image is one of self-containment, of regal self-assurance. A little on the lines of the late actress Suchitra Sen, she has cut her friends off from her life. What a long journey it has been for her. Rekha is a survivor. She fiercely fought back every single time she was down and out. She got up without help every time she fell. Perhaps history will be kinder to her than people have been.

'I am and I will always be Bhanurekha. I don't think people change. She was a very shy, very loving loner, which I still am,' said Rekha.[10]

Epilogue

It was 8 January 2016. The night of the Star Screen Awards in Bombay, a glamorous industry gathering. On that night something happened that was beyond anyone's imagination.

Amitabh and Jaya were watching the function seated in the front row. Some six or seven seats down, also in the front row, was seated Rekha with her secretary Farzana. She looked magnificent wearing a golden Kanjeevaram sari, and with sindoor in her hair.

Towards the end of the function, the best actor award was announced: Amitabh Bachchan got it for his performance in the film *Piku* (2015). As soon as Amitabh got up and headed towards the stage to take his award, Rekha made her way towards Jaya, greeted her with an embrace, and took Amitabh's seat.

Amitabh was given a standing ovation, and Jaya and Rekha also joined the audience and stood up together as a gesture of admiration and respect for the superstar. Rekha whispered something in Jaya's ears. They both smiled. And then, their eyes turned towards Amitabh, and rested on the man who has been an important and indispensable part of their lives for decades.

Rekha and Jaya stood together applauding Amitabh, their eyes fixed on him, smiles enlivening their faces.

Notes

1. 'Basera'

1. *Filmfare*, April 1990
2. Author's interview with Neeraj Kumar
3. 'Mukesh: Rags to Rekha', *Filmfare*, April 1990
4. 'Rekha: Her Story', *Filmfare*, December 1990
5. Rauf Ahmed's interview with Rekha, 'I Didn't Kill Mukesh', *Filmfare*, December 1990
6. 'Rekha: Her Story', *Filmfare*, December 1990
7. 'Rekha: Her Story', *Filmfare*, December 1990
8. 'Rekha: Her Story', *Filmfare*, December 1990
9. Interview with Deepti Naval, *Filmfare*, April 1990
10. 'Rekha: Her Story', *Filmfare*, December 1990

2. Divorce

1. Author's interview with Neeraj Kumar
2. 'The Tragedy That Was Unnecessary', *Stardust*, November 1990

3. 'The Tragedy That Was Unnecessary', *Stardust*, November 1990
4. Author's interview with Neeraj Kumar
5. Interview with Rekha, 'Rekha on the Romance of Being Married…', *Filmfare*, April 1990
6. Interview with Rekha, 'Rekha on the Romance of Being Married…', *Filmfare*, April 1990
7. Interview with Rekha, 'Rekha on the Romance of Being Married…', *Filmfare*, April 1990
8. Author's interview with Neeraj Kumar
9. 'Rekha: Her Story', *Filmfare*, December 1990
10. 'Rekha: Her Story', *Filmfare*, December 1990
11. *Stardust*, June 1990
12. Interview with Deepti Naval, 'The Tragedy That Was Unnecessary', *Stardust*, November 1990
13. 'Rekha: Her Story', *Filmfare*, December 1990

3. Witch Hunt

1. 'The Macabre Truth behind Mukesh's Suicide', *Cine Blitz*, November 1990
2. *The Times of India*, 4 October 1990
3. 'The Tragedy That Was Unnecessary', *Stardust*, November 1990
4. 'The Macabre Truth behind Mukesh's Suicide', *Cine Blitz*, November 1990
5. Nishi Prem's interview with Deepti Naval, *Stardust*, November 1990
6. Nishi Prem's interview with Subhash Ghai, *Stardust*,

November 1990

7. Nishi Prem's interview with Anupam Kher, *Stardust*, November 1990

4. The Beginning

1. Narayani Ganesh, *Eternal Romantic: My Father, Gemini Ganesan*, Delhi: Roli (2010)

5. Bhanurekha

1. Cited in Mohan Deep, *Eurekha! The Intimate Life Story of Rekha*, Bombay: Shivani Publications (1999)
2. 'Rekha: On Women She Admires', *Movie*, May 1987
3. Narayani Ganesh, *Eternal Romantic: My Father, Gemini Ganesan*, Delhi: Roli (2010)
4. *Bombay Magazine*, 7 January 1986

6. Bollywood Debut

1. Jitendra Kothari's interview with Kuljeet Pal, 1979
2. 'Rekha: Images of a Perfect World', *Movie*, June 1986
3. Simi Garewal's interview with Rekha, *Rendezvous with Simi Garewal*, June 2004
4. Author's interview with Jerry Pinto
5. Cited in Mohan Deep, *Eurekha! The Intimate Life Story of Rekha*, Bombay: Shivani Publications (1999)
6. Dinesh Raheja, 'Rekha: The Divine Diva', rediff.com, 17 May 2003, http://www.rediff.com/movies/report/

dinesh/20030517.htm

7. 'The Diva Rules', *Telegraph*, 3 August 2008

7. The Kiss of 'Life'

1. Dinesh Raheja, '25 Years of a Special Woman', *Movie*, October 1994
2. Cited in Mohan Deep, *Eurekha! The Intimate Life Story of Rekha*, Bombay: Shivani Publications (1999)
3. Jitendra Kothari's interview with Kuljeet Pal, 1979
4. Author's interview with Jerry Pinto

8. 'Madrasan'

1. Author's interview with Shyam Benegal
2. Dinesh Raheja, '25 Years of a Special Woman', *Movie*, October 1994
3. Dinesh Raheja, '25 Years of a Special Woman', *Movie*, October 1994
4. Dinesh Raheja, '25 Years of a Special Woman', *Movie*, October 1994
5. Dinesh Raheja, 'Rekha: The Divine Diva', rediff.com, 17 May 2003, http://www.rediff.com/movies/report/dinesh/20030517.htm

9. Vin Vin and Kin Kin

1. Interview with Rekha, *Stardust*, September 1972
2. Interview with Rekha, *Stardust*, September 1972

3. Interview with Rekha, *Stardust*, September 1972
4. Cited in Mohan Deep, *Eurekha! The Intimate Life Story of Rekha*, Bombay: Shivani Publications (1999)
5. Interview with Rekha, *Stardust*, September 1972
6. Interview with Rekha, *Stardust*, September 1973
7. Simi Garewal's interview with Rekha, *Rendezvous with Simi Garewal*, June 2004
8. Interview with Yogita Bali, 'Rekha: The Eternal "Other Woman"', *Super*, March 1979
9. *Super*, June 1980
10. *Stardust*, April 1975

10. Didibai

1. *Super*, June 1980
2. Cited in Mohan Deep, *Eurekha! The Intimate Life Story of Rekha*, Bombay: Shivani Publications (1999)

11. Makeover

1. Author's interview with Khalid Mohamed
2. Dinesh Raheja, '25 Years of a Special Woman', *Movie*, October 1994
3. *The Best of Stardust*, Vol. 2, 1981
4. Bhawana Somaaya's interview with Rekha, May 1987
5. Bharati S. Pradhan, 'When Big B Was Banned', *Telegraph*, 28 June 2015, http://www.telegraphindia.com/1150628/jsp/7days/story_28212.jsp
6. Amitabh Bachchan, 'Day 1740', *Bachchan Bol*, 20/21 January

2013, http://srbachchan.tumblr.com/post/41048390032
7. *Super*, June 1980
8. 'Beautiful but Doomed: Rekha's Personal Crisis', *Stardust*, February 1982
9. *Stardust*, September 1976

12. Ghar

1. Author's interview with Gulzar
2. Cited in Mohan Deep, *Eurekha! The Intimate Life Story of Rekha*, Bombay: Shivani Publications (1999)

13. Zohrabai

1. Mohan Deep, *Eurekha! The Intimate Life Story of Rekha*, Bombay: Shivani Publications (1999)
2. Dinesh Raheja, '25 Years of a Special Woman', *Movie*, October 1994
3. Interview with Rekha, 'Rekha: Girl without a Conscience?' *Best of Stardust*, 1978
4. 'Rekha: Girl without a Conscience?', *Best of Stardust*, 1978
5. 'Rekha: Girl without a Conscience?', *Best of Stardust*, 1978
6. 'Rekha: Girl without a Conscience?', *Best of Stardust*, 1978
7. 'Rekha: Girl without a Conscience?', *Best of Stardust*, 1978

14. The Other Woman

1. Mohan Deep, *Eurekha! The Intimate Life Story of Rekha*, Bombay: Shivani Publications (1999)

2. 'Why Men Adore Rekha... and Women Pity Her!', *Stardust*, December 1976

3. Interview with Zeenat Aman, *Stardust*, December 1976

4. 'Why Men Adore Rekha...and Women Pity Her!', *Stardust*, December 1976

5. 'Filmi Farce of the Year: How Two Women Stooped to Save the Man They Share', *Stardust*, 1981

6. Mohan Deep, *Eurekha! The Intimate Life Story of Rekha*, Bombay: Shivani Publications (1999)

7. Mohan Deep, *Eurekha! The Intimate Life Story of Rekha*, Bombay: Shivani Publications (1999)

8. 'Rekha: Girl without a Conscience?', *Best of Stardust*, 1978

15. Queen

1. Bunny Reuben, 'The Double Standards of the Indian Actress', *Star & Style*, 2 May 1980

2. Author's interview with Gulzar

3. Author's interview with Saawan Kumar

16. 'Silsila'

1. 'Filmi Farce of the Year: How Two Women Stooped to Save the Man They Share', *Stardust*, 1981

2. 'Jaya Is Back', *Super*, November 1980

3. 'Filmi Farce of the Year: How Two Women Stooped to Save the Man They Share', *Stardust*, 1981

4. Author's interview with Sagar Sarhadi

5. 'Jaya Is Back', *Super*, November 1980

6. 'Rekha on Women She Admires', *Movie*, May 1987

17. Love Triangle

1. *Super*, May 1981
2. Sonia Deol's interview with Yash Chopra, BBC Asia, 11 August 2010
3. 'Inside the Making of *Silsila*', *Cine Blitz*, August 1981
4. 'Inside the Making of *Silsila*', *Cine Blitz*, August 1981
5. Dinesh Raheja, '25 Years of a Special Woman', *Movie*, October 1994
6. Tejaswini Ganti, *Producing Bollywood: Inside the Contemporary Hindi Film Industry*, London: Duke University Press Books (2012)
7. Mohan Deep, *Eurekha! The Intimate Life Story of Rekha*, Bombay: Shivani Publications (1999)

18. Accident

1. *Filmfare*, November 1984
2. Puneet Issar, 'Puneet Relax, It Was an Accident', rediff.com, 11 October 2002, http://www.rediff.com/entertai/2002/oct/11puneet.htm
3. Mohan Deep, *Eurekha! The Intimate Life Story of Rekha*, Bombay: Shivani Publications (1999)
4. *Movie*, September 1982
5. *Filmfare*, November 1984
6. Puneet Issar, 'Puneet Relax, It Was an Accident', rediff.com, 11 October 2002, http://www.rediff.com/entertai/2002/

oct/11puneet.htm

7. *Filmfare*, November 1984
8. Mohan Deep, *Eurekha! The Intimate Life Story of Rekha*, Bombay: Shivani Publications (1999)
9. *Filmfare*, November 1984
10. Mohan Deep, *Eurekha! The Intimate Life Story of Rekha*, Bombay: Shivani Publications (1999)
11. *Filmfare*, November 1984

19. Umrao

1. Interview with Farooq Sheikh, 'You Will Always Remember the Old *Umrao Jaan*', rediff.com, 6 November 2006, http://www.rediff.com/movies/2006/nov/06farooq.htm
2. Roshmila Bhattacharya, 'In Focus: Poetry, Pain, Passion and Rekha,' *Mumbai Mirror*, 14 April 2015

20. Arthouse

1. Author's interview with Shyam Benegal
2. Author's interview with Shyam Benegal
3. Author's interview with Shyam Benegal
4. Author's interview with Ramesh Talwar
5. Author's interview with Gulzar
6. Author's interview with Shekhar Suman

21. 'Lady Amitabh'

1. Harneet Singh, 'Gulzar Is Always Looking for the Right *Lafz*', *Mint Lounge*, 6 May 2016
2. M.L. Dhawan, 'Year of Offbeat Films', *Sunday Tribune*, 18 August 2002

22. Suicide

1. Rauf Ahmed's interview with Rekha, 'I Didn't Kill Mukesh', *Filmfare*, December 1990
2. Rauf Ahmed's interview with Rekha, 'I Didn't Kill Mukesh', *Filmfare*, December 1990
3. 'The Macabre Truth behind Mukesh's Suicide', *Cine Blitz*, November 1990
4. R.K. Mehta and B. Viswas's interview with Anil Gupta, 'Anil Bhai Re-lives…', *Cine Blitz*, November 1990
5. 'The Macabre Truth behind Mukesh's Suicide', *Cine Blitz*, November 1990
6. R.K. Mehta and B. Viswas's interview with Anil Gupta, 'Anil Bhai Re-lives…', *Cine Blitz*, November 1990
7. Author's interview with Neeraj Kumar
8. Simi Garewal's interview with Rekha, *Rendezvous with Simi Garewal*, June 2004

23. Orphaned

1. Prem Panicker, 'The Magic That Is Rekha', rediff.com, 10 October 2003, http://www.rediff.com/movies/2003/oct/10rekha.htm

2. Author's interview with Tej Sapru
3. Jitesh Pillai's interview with Rekha, 2 December 2011, http://www.idiva.com/news-entertainment/rekha-i-have-received-enough-love-to-let-go/9415
4. Author's interview with Jerry Pinto

24. Afterlife

1. Rekhathediva.com
2. Author's interview with Khalid Mohamed
3. Simi Garewal's interview with Amitabh Bachchan, *Rendezvous with Simi Garewal*, 1998

25. Rajya Sabha

1. Author's interview with Amar Singh

26. Farzana

1. Malavika Sangghvi, 'Deconstructing Rekha', *Business Standard*, 5 May 2012
2. Dinesh Raheja, '25 Years of a Special Woman', *Movie*, October 1994
3. Author's interview with Dinesh Raheja
4. 'Rekha Was Ego Trip for Amitabh', *Times of India*, 16 September 2009
5. Malavika Sangghvi, 'Deconstructing Rekha', *Business Standard*, 5 May 2012

6. Rauf Ahmed's interview with Rekha, 'I Didn't Kill Mukesh', *Filmfare*, December 1990
7. Author's interview with Jerry Pinto
8. *Filmfare*, November 1984
9. *Filmfare*, November 1984
10. Simi Garewal's interview with Rekha, *Rendezvous with Simi Garewal*, June 2004

Acknowledgements

Shazi Zaman, s*hukriya* for motivating me and making me believe that I could do it.

Gulzar, Shyam Benegal, Muzaffar Ali, Khalid Mohamed and Jerry Pinto, for sharing their memories and sharp observations.

Chiki Sarkar for her enthusiasm for the idea and decision to stand by it.

Bikram Grewal for his casual reference that turned into a serious book.

Neeraj Kumar for his immense help in joining the dots and being ever supportive.

Mrs Mala Kumar for the wonderful pictures from her personal album and her love.

Sumant Batra for letting me into a piece of his heart: Chitrashala Museum.

Puneet Sharma, whose sea-facing house in Mumbai became home during my visits to Mumbai for the extensive research this book entailed.

Acknowledgements

Namita Gokhale for graciously allowing me to use photographs from her wonderful magazine, *Super*.

Manav Manglani for sportingly allowing me to use a photograph from his collection.

Apurva Jadhav for stepping into my shoes and making multiple trips to the National Archives, without ever complaining. I'll be ever grateful.

Saumya Kulshreshtha for adopting this book as her very own pet project and spending innumerable hours reading and rereading every line and refining the text.

The brilliant team at Juggernaut, with a special shout-out to my editor Parth Mehrotra for marshalling the narrative to this form. Renu Agal for championing the idea and always standing by me.

Various co-stars of Rekha, technicians and film-makers, some of who wish to remain unnamed, for adding significant layers to Rekha's life and times.

Several friends and well-wishers who helped at crucial moments: Shekhar Suman, Pavan Jha, Mohan Deep, Rasheed Kidwai, Hanif Zaveri, Tej Sapru, Suparna Sharma, Richa Thakur, Shruti Bhatt, Bharathi S. Pradhan, Deeptakirti Chaudhuri, Shabry Bakshi, the late Sushama Shelly, Malvika Verma, Dinesh Raheja, Ajay Khullar, Ashish Kumar Singh and Arnab Banerjee.

Milind Khandekar for allowing me access to the archives at ABP News. Rajnish Ahuja for helping me out with pictures.

Acknowledgements

Anant Bansal, Ankita Kumar, Vishal Gaurav and Rohit Lal for their unconditional support, always.

My eternal gratitude goes to my family: M. Usman, Haseeba Khanam, Sahir and Atiya.

To Pervez Jamal and Shabnam Faridi for their love and encouragement.

And, lastly, heartfelt thanks to my wife, Nazia Erum, for her advice, her patience and her love. And to my little angel Myra for always making me smile, despite this book getting much of the time that was supposed to be for her.

Index

Aaj Ka Mahatma, 97
Aap Ki Khatir, 94
Aandhi, 100
Aastha, 186
Ab Insaaf Hoga, 184
Abbas, Khwaja Ahmad, 43, 51, 73, 79
Adalat, 86
Agarwal, Mukesh, 2–8, 14–17, 21, 170–78
  confession, 9–10
  depression, 10–12, 19–20
  divorce, 20
  estrangement, 16–18
  suicide, 21–25, 170
  suicide attempt, 19–20
  wedding, 12–13
Ahimsa, 110
Ahmad, Sultan, 93
Alaap, 92, 94–95, 118
Ali, Muzaffar, 109, 146–54

Aman, Zeenat, 109, 112, 117
Amar Akbar Anthony, 94
Amitabh: The Making of a Superstar, 192
Anand, Dev, 29, 62–63
Anand, Tinnu, 126, 168
Anand, Vijay, 109
Angulimaal, 67
Anjana Safar, 41, 44, 46, 49, 53
Anokhi Ada, 66
Aradhana, 43
Astaire, Fred, 202
Azaad Desh Ke Gulam, 12–13
Azmi, Shabana, 109, 154, 193–94

Babbar, Raj, 155, 162, 181–82
Babi, Parveen, 117, 125
Bachchan, Abhishek, 192
Bachchan, Aishwarya, 192
Bachchan, Amitabh, 10, 44,

72, 79–86, 90–95, 102, 106,
110–11, 113–16, 122–38,
144, 146–47, 162, 168, 183,
187–90, 192–94, 198–99,
204–05
accident, 138–43
Bachchan, Harivansh Rai, 79
Bachchan, Jaya (nee Bhaduri),
63, 78–81, 83, 93, 102,
106–08, 113–16, 123–24,
126–37, 140–41, 143–44,
193–95, 204–05
statements, 144–45
Bachchan, Teji, 113
Bachke Rehna Re Baba, 191
Bahurani, 170
Bajaj, Akash, 10–12, 21, 24, 173
Bajaj, Anjali, 11
Bajaj, Monisha, 11
Balasaraswathi, Surabhi, 32
Bali, Yogita, 73, 198
Banu, Saira, 43
Baseraa, 118, 157
Bedi, Kabir, 167
Bedi, Protima, 113
Benegal, Shyam, 55–56, 109,
154–56, 186
Bewakoof, 67
Bharat Ki Nari, 25, 175
Bhattacharya, Basu, 186
Bhonsle, Asha, 152
Bhoot, 191

Bhrashtachar, 170
Bigg Boss, 142
Biswajeet, 41, 48–49
Biwi Ho Toh Aisi, 166
Bodas, Sanjay, 7
Bokadia, K.C., 175

Chakkar Pe Chakkar, 94
Charaborty, Mithun, 170
Chandra, N., 166
Chatterjee, Manek, 98
Chatterjee, Moushumi, 70
Chatterjee, Ritesh, 70
Chawla, Juhi, 166, 169
Chennai, 1, 27
Chopra, Pamela, 136
Chopra, Prem, 82, 85, 176
Chopra, Yash, 122–23, 125–27,
130–31, 137
Cine Blitz, 24, 91, 113, 132, 134
Clerk, 169
Coolie, 138, 142–43, 162

Daasi, 129–30
Dafaa, 302, 82
Damini, 184
Dasgupta, Sushmita, 192–93,
199
Deewar, 83–84, 86
Desai, Manmohan, 111, 113,
138
Desh Premee, 138

Index

Dharam Karam, 83

Dharmatma, 74, 82

Dharmendra, 8, 63, 72, 81, 110–11, 115, 117, 169

Dhawan, M.L., 164, 167

Dhillion, Poonam, 125

Dildaar, 94

Dixit, Madhuri, 166

Do Anjaane, 81–86, 97, 199

Do Aur Do Paanch, 123

Do Boond Paani, 73

Do Shikari, 46

Don, 110

Dost, 81

Dostana, 123

Duniya Ka Mela, 79–80

Dushman, 81

Dutt, Guru, 50–51

Dutt, Nargis, 51, 109, 112, 194

Dutt, Sanjay, 162

Dutt, Sunil, 18, 79, 111

Ek Bechara, 65–66

Ek Hi Bhool, 118

Ek Hi Raasta, 94, 97

Ek Thi Rita, 67

Elaan, 64

En Purushanthaan Enakku Mattumthaan, 19

Eurekha, 92

Faasle, 166

Farishta Ya Qatil, 94, 97

Farz, 65

Farzana, 18, 25, 172–73, 196, 200–01, 204

film censorship, 51–52

Film City, 134

Film World, 86

Filmfare, 141, 144, 165, 171

Free Love, 73

Gaal Gulaabi Nain Sharaabi, 73

Galiyon Ka Raja, 40

Gandhi, Indira, 91, 140, 168

Gandhi, Rajiv, 15, 140, 168

Gandhi, Sonia, 194

Ganesan, Alamelu 'Bobji', 30, 34

Ganesan, Gemini (Ramaswamy), 13, 28–32, 34–35, 37, 45, 179

Ganesan, Savithri, 32–33

Ganesh, Narayani, 27, 29–30, 32, 34–35

Eternal Romantic: My Father, Gemini Ganesan, 34

Ganga Ki Saugandh, 93

Garewal, Simi, 53, 87, 96, 174, 188, 201

Rendezvous with Simi Garewal, 187

Geetanjali, 184

Gemini Studios, 27, 40
Ghai, Subhash, 25
Ghar, 97–101, 120, 158, 164
Ghosh, B.N., 65
Guddi, 63
Guha, Dulal, 81–82, 86, 199
Gulzar, 98–100, 120, 154, 157–58, 164–65
Gulzar, Meghna, 158
Gulzar, Rakhee, 100, 102, 104, 158, 183
Gupta, Anil, 5, 14, 17, 21–22, 24, 173
Gupta, Nihar Ranjan, 81

Haasan, Kamal, 162
Haseenon Ka Devta, 47, 64
Hawas, 121
Helen, 94
Hema Malini, 8, 40, 62, 83, 109, 115, 117, 183, 193
Hussain, Tahir, 129–30

Ijaazat, 158, 164–66
Immaan Dharam, 92, 94–95
India Today, 156
Indian New Wave movement, 154
Insaf Ki Devi, 25, 184
Insaniyat, 29
Issar, Puneet, 139, 142–43

Jaal, 166
Jaani Dushman, 110
Jayanthi, A.T., 115
Jayshree, T., 56, 58–59
Jeetendra, 19, 23, 65–67, 111, 118
Jeevan, 73–76
Jeevan Dhaara, 181–82
Johar, I.S., 67
Johny Mera Naam, 62
Judaai, 118
Jungle Mein Mangal, 73
Junoon, 155

Kaala Patthar, 123
Kaaliya, 126, 138
Kabhi Kabhie, 86
Kachcha Chor, 94, 97
Kahani Kismat Ki, 72
Kajol, 185
Kal, Aaj Aur Kal, 52
Kalyug, 56, 109, 154–57
Kama Sutra, 186
Kapadia, Dimple, 112, 130
Kapoor, Anil, 166
Kapoor, Jennifer, 61
Kapoor, Prithviraj, 194
Kapoor, Raj, 62, 83
Kapoor, Randhir, 52, 83, 96
Kapoor, Rishi, 113–14
Kapoor, Shashi, 55, 61, 94, 154–55, 158–62, 169, 171

Kapoor, Shekhar, 166
Karnad, Girish, 155, 158–60
Kartavya, 110
Kasam Suhaag Ki, 169
Kasme Vaade, 102–03
Kaur, Prakash, 115
Kaur, Surinder, 4–8
Keemat, 72, 110
Khambatta, Persis, 53
Khan, Aamir, 129, 166
Khan, Akbar, 8
Khan, Amjad, 103
Khan, Feroz, 3, 74, 83
Khan, Mansoor, 166
Khan, Salman, 166
Khan, Sanjay, 3, 8, 47, 64, 80
Khan, Shah Rukh, 125–26, 132
Khanna, Rajesh, 43, 72, 79, 81, 112, 130, 169, 194
Khanna, Vinod, 64, 104
Khayyam, 152
Kher, Anupam, 23, 25
Khiladiyon Ka Khiladi, 185
Khoobsurat, 107, 109, 117–20, 158, 164, 167, 200
Khoon Bhari Maang, 166–67, 169, 183
Khoon Pasina, 92, 94–95, 110, 199
Khosla, G.D., 51

Khosla Committee, 51–52
Khuddar, 138
Kidwai, Rasheed, 191, 194
Kolhapure, Padmini, 125
Krishna, Gopi, 152
Krrish, 191
Kudiyon Ka Hai Zamana, 191
Kumar, Akshay, 185
Kumar, Dilip, 29, 135
Kumar, Kiran, 73–77
Kumar, Kishore, 45, 67
Kumar, Manoj, 169
Kumar, Neeraj, 2–3, 10–12, 14, 19, 22–24, 174
Kumar, Rajeev, 162
Kumar, Rajendra, 120
Kumar, Rakesh, 95, 110–11
Kumar, Saawan, 67–68, 118, 120–21, 169, 186
Kumar, Sanjeev, 129, 134, 136
Kumar, Shiv, 75
Kumari, Meena, 45, 90, 197–98

Laawaris, 124, 138
Lajja, 191
Lakhia, Kumudini, 152
Life, 52–53
Locket, 129–30
Loren, Sophia, 198

Maang Bharo Sajna, 118
Madam X, 184

Mahaan, 138
Mahboob Studio, 49
Malkan, Kitty, 10, 17
Manampol Mangalyam, 32
Manobala, 18
Manzur, 152
Mehmaan, 47
Mehmood, 80, 135
Mehra, Kamla, 68–71
Mehra, Kiran, 121
Mehra, Prakash, 92, 104, 124, 141
Mehra, Sharda, 69
Mehra, Umesh, 185
Mehra, Vinod, 64, 67–72, 74, 76–77, 98, 100–01, 120–21
Mera Pati Sirf Mera Hai, 18
Miss Malini, 28
Mitho Bhabhi (Anil Gupta's wife), 5, 24, 173, 196
Mohamed, Khalid, 89, 186, 197
Mother, 186
Mother India, 184
Movie, 114, 141, 143, 198
Mr India, 166
Mr Natwarlal, 110
Mudaliyar, Varadarajan, 140
Mughal–E–Azam, 152
Mukherjee, Hrishikesh, 63, 72, 79, 92, 109, 117–19, 199
Mukherjee, Shomu, 130
Mumbai, 1

Mumtaz, 40, 43, 60, 82
Muqaddar Ka Sikandar, 92, 102, 104, 107, 110, 150, 181, 197

Nag, Anant, 155
Nagina, 23
Nair, Mira, 186
Nair, Vijay, 155
Namak Halal, 138
Namak Haraam, 72, 79, 118
Narayan, R.K., 28, 51
Nastic, 138
Natraj Studio, 124
Naval, Deepti, 6, 8, 18, 25
Nawathe, Raja, 49
Nellie, 124, 129
Nihalani, Govind, 109, 154
Nischol, Navin, 57–58, 60, 62–63
Noorie, 184
Nutan, 120

Paisa Ya Pyaar, 41
Pal, Kuljeet, 40–42, 44–50, 53
Pal, Shatrujeet, 44, 47
Pandey, Snehlata, 114–15
Panicker, Prem, 176–77
Parekh, Asha, 43
Parineeta, 191
Parmatma, 97
Parveen, Begum Abida, 196
Patel, Anuradha, 165

Pathak, Dina, 151
Patil, Smita, 109, 125, 128, 154
Phool Bane Angaray, 175–77, 183, 200
Piku, 204
Pinto, Jerry, 46, 50–51, 61, 104, 111, 128, 181–83, 185, 201
Ponti, Carlo, 198
Pradhan, Bharathi S., 181
Pushpavalli, 13, 28–34, 36–42, 44–46, 56–57, 66, 69, 93, 178–80
  Babuji, 28, 36
  Dhanalakshmi, 33, 173, 179
  Radha, 33, 35, 173, 181
  Rama, 28, 36
  Seshu, 33
Prakash, K., 33
Premendra, 64
Prithvi Theatre, 159
Pyar Ki Jeet, 166

Qayamat Se Qayamat Tak, 166
Qila, 186

R.K. Studio, 52, 113–14
Raagini, 67
Raaj Kumar, 40, 46, 74
Radhika, 19
Raheja, Dinesh, 104, 198
Rahu Ketu, 97
Rai, Gulshan, 130

Rajadhyaksha, Gautam, 185
Ram Balram, 109, 123
Ram Bharose, 94, 97
Ram Dada, 90, 198
Ram Kasam, 97
Rama Rao, T., 118
Ramanaidu, D., 59
Ramani, Bina, 3–5
Rampur Ka Lakshman, 72, 90
Rangula Ratnam, 34
Rao, Raghavendra, 13
Reddy, Neelam Sanjiva, 115
Rehman, Waheeda, 43, 50–51
Rekha, 3–4, 10–12, 16, 23, 34, 71–72, 95, 109
  AB's influence, 83, 86–93, 198–200
  acting tradition, 156
  ad films, 55
  and AB, 84–87, 91–96, 101, 103, 106–08, 116, 120, 123–24, 131–32, 137, 140–47, 187–90, 192–94, 198–200, 202, 204–05
  and costume, 150, 167–68
  and Didibhai, 79, 87, 93, 129, 133
  and father, 33
  and kathak, 152–53
  and looks, 46–47, 57–61
  and make-up, 89–90

and mother, 180
and press, 53–54, 62, 64, 72,
    76–77
as an actress, 78–80, 96, 100,
    117, 122, 154, 165
award ceremonies, 192
    Filmfare Awards
        function, 192
    Star Screen Awards, 204
awards, 114
    Filmfare Award, 120,
        179, 186
    Filmfare lifetime
        achievement award,
        186
    National Award, 152
'Basera', 2, 5, 21
Bhanurekha Ganesan, 1, 28,
    30–33, 35–39, 41–44,
    47, 203
birth, 32, 76
buying a flat, 78
courtship, 4–5
critical acclaim, 156–57
denial, 72
divorce, 20
early years, 27, 30–37
entry into films, 37–39
    exploitation, 45–46, 49
    Hindi cinema, 41–46
fashion photoshoots, 184–
    85

financial responsibilities, 40,
    42–43, 180–81
fresh start, 174–76
heartache, 66–67, 76
humiliation, 71
image, 112–13, 145, 186
in *Silsila*, 126–36
income tax raid, 161
interviews, 83–84, 90, 106–
    07, 145, 153, 171–72,
    177, 202
'Lady Amitabh', 166–67,
    200
language flair, 41–42, 60
loneliness, 59–60
made fun of, 59
makeover, 88–90, 97, 103,
    197
marital problems, 14–18
marriage, 70–71, 170–72
married life, 13–14
negative press, 24–26, 143–
    44, 171–72
on–screen kiss, 48–54
playing a courtesan, 104–05,
    147–53, 158, 182, 197
poise, 59–62
popularity, 64
positive press, 86, 156–57
professionalism, 157, 161
Rajya Sabha, 194–95
recluse, 178–79

romantic relationships, 66–67, 70, 74–77, 84–85, 106, 111
rumours, 162–63
scandalous past, 75–76
'sex kitten', 50, 64, 99, 112
sindoor, 113–15
suicide attempt, 36, 70, 77
views on sex, 68–69, 77
wedding, 6–8, 12–13
when in love, 74–75, 92
widowhood, 23–26, 171, 174
Reuben, Bunny, 119–20
Rogers, Ginger, 202
Roshan, G.M., 80
Roshan, Rakesh, 166–67, 191
Ruswa, Mirza Hadi, 148

Saajan Ki Saheli, 118, 120
Saal Solvan Chadya, 94
Saat Hindustani, 43, 79
Saaz Aur Sanam, 64
Sahni, Balraj, 51
Sangghvi, Malavika, 185, 200–01
Sansar, 29, 162, 166
Santoshi, Raj Kumar, 191
Sapno Ka Saudagar, 62
Sapru, Tej, 173,179–80
Sarhadi, Sagar, 127–28
Satte Pe Satta, 138

Sawan Bhadon, 47, 56–61, 110
Scindia, Madhavrao, 16
Sehgal, Mohan, 47, 56–57, 60, 110
Sen, Suchitra, 202
Seshadri, Meenakshi, 169
Shah, Naseeruddin, 148, 164–65
Shahenshah, 168
Shakti, 138
Sheikh, Farooq, 148–49, 151–52
Shepherd, James, 52
Sheshnaag, 18, 23, 26
Sheth, Jayesh, 184–85
Shobha, 66
Sholay, 86, 169
Showtime, 24
Silsila, 116, 122–38, 157, 188
Singh, Amar, 193
Singh, Harneet, 165
Singh, Khushwant, 112–13
Singh, Neetu, 50, 113–14
Singh, Shailendra, 162
Sinha, Shatrughan, 81
Sippy, N.N., 98
Sippy, Ramesh, 170
Somayya, Bhawana, 76, 90
Souten, 169
Souten Ki Beti, 120–21, 169
Sridevi, 23, 166, 169
Sriniwas, N., 74

Star & Style, 68, 91, 115
Stardust, 19, 91, 106, 114–16, 124
Suhaag, 110–11, 181
Suman, Shekhar, 159–60
Super, 128
Super Nani, 142, 191

Tagore, Sharmila, 43, 82
Talwar, Ramesh, 118, 157
Tezaab, 166
Thakur, Dinesh, 99
Trehan, Madhu, 156

Udaan, 184
Umrao Jaan, 103, 109, 114, 143, 146–47, 151–52, 154, 157, 197, 200
Umrao Jaan Ada, 148
Utsav, 155, 158–61

Vasan, S.S., 28, 30
Vanisri, 41
Verma, Ram Gopal, 191
Vijeta, 109, 155
Vyjayanthimala, 45

Walia, Sonu, 166, 168
Wo Mai Nahi, 82

Yeh Aag Kab Bhujhegi, 18
YouTube, 80

Zameen Aasmaan, 162, 166
Zanjeer, 80
Zaveri, Hanif, 80
Zorro, 82
Zubeidaa, 186

A Note on the Author

Yasser Usman is an award-winning TV journalist and the author of the bestselling *Rajesh Khanna: The Untold Story of India's First Superstar.*

THE APP
FOR INDIAN
READERS

Fresh, original books tailored for mobile and for India. Starting at ₹10.

juggernaut.in

1

CRAFTED FOR MOBILE READING

Thought you would never read a book on mobile? Let us prove you wrong.

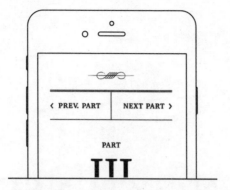

Beautiful Typography

The quality of print transferred
to your mobile. Forget ugly PDFs.

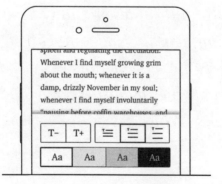

Customizable Reading

Read in the font size, spacing
and background of your liking.

AN EXTENSIVE LIBRARY

Including fresh, new, original Juggernaut books from the likes of Sunny Leone, Praveen Swami, Husain Haqqani, Umera Ahmed, Rujuta Diwekar and lots more. Plus, books from partner publishers and loads of free classics. Whichever genre you like, there's a book waiting for you.

DON'T JUST READ; INTERACT

We're changing the reading experience from passive to active.

Ask authors questions

Get all your answers from the horse's mouth.
Juggernaut authors actually reply to every
question they can.

Rate and review

Let everyone know of your favourite reads or
critique the finer points of a book – you will be
heard in a community of like-minded readers.

Gift books to friends

For a book-lover, there's no nicer gift than
a book personally picked. You can even
do it anonymously if you like.

Enjoy new book formats

Discover serials released in parts over
time, picture books including comics,
and story-bundles at discounted rates.
And coming soon, audiobooks.

4

LOWEST PRICES & ONE-TAP BUYING

Books start at ₹10 with regular discounts and free previews.